The Use and Abuse of Books

The Use and Abuse of Books

De Commodis litterarum atque incommodis

Translation and Introduction by Renée Neu Watkins

For information about this book, write or call:
  Waveland Press, Inc.
  P.O. Box 400
  Prospect Heights, Illinois 60070
  (847) 634-0081

Cover: The hands of John writing the Apocalypse. Detail from Hans Memling's altarpiece, 1479. Bruges, St. John's Hospital.

Copyright © 1999 by Renée Neu Watkins

ISBN 1-57766-049-8

All rights reserved. No part of this book may be reproduced, stored in a retrieval system, or transmitted in any form or by any means without permission in writing from the publisher.

Printed in the United States of America

7   6   5   4   3   2   1

Introduction

De Commodis litterarum atque incommodis,[1] literally translated, is *Advantages and Disadvantages of Letters*; less literally but true to the spirit of the work, it can be translated *The Use and Abuse of Books*. Hereinafter, for convenience, the treatise will be referred to as *Use of Books*. In fifteenth-century Latin *litterae*, as in archaic English, "letters" refers not only to the basic unit of written language but also to documents and books, to an education focused on reading and writing, to Latin texts in particular, and to the creation as well as the consumption of literature in general. In this treatise, it usually refers to a rhetorical and philosophical education, particularly one pursued beyond the point where it is a prerequisite to professional training. Such an education, Alberti implies, includes psychology and astronomy as well as classical philosophy. In certain parts of the treatise, by contrast, litterae refers precisely to education in law, medicine, and theology.

What Alberti discusses, however, is not the content of an education, but the results, the outcome in a cost-benefit sense. There are heavy costs to the individual and, he contends, even if one chooses a career in law or medicine, no worldly advantages at all. For the world the results of an individual acquiring knowledge from books are of inestimable value, but the world does not reward him. Neither the professions nor teaching at any level make men prosperous and respected. What scholarly activity does do is wear out the student with anxiety and labor, unless, Alberti says, one perverts erudition to serve the selfish and often criminal purposes of other men, and even then one is likely to remain poor. Therefore, to seek worldly advantages from one's pursuit of learning, as many do, is both unethical and almost always futile. Alberti moves back and forth between attacks on the pomposity and careerism of scholars who have, as it were, sold out, and lamentations

1

concerning the cruelty of the world to those scholars who are honest and serious. Throughout the treatise he suggests that intellectuals often deceive themselves as to their own needs and purposes.

Alberti's ostensible aim is to free students from the comfortable illusions they may have when setting out on an academic path and to discourage those who set out on that path precisely in order to achieve wealth and status. At the same time, the treatise encourages the serious student, praising the wisdom said to reside in books, considering lifelong devotion to study a high virtue, and asserting that, for spiritual reasons, it is well worth the sacrifice it entails.

The Use and Abuse of Books seems an appropriate title. If incidentally this English title reminds us of Nietzsche,[2] we may note that Nietzsche, too, was full of scorn for "the world" and that his vision of the superior man was influenced by the Renaissance via Burckhardt, whose description of the Renaissance man was based especially on Alberti. The notion of a superior man in lonely opposition to the general and hypocritical scramble for advantage, and of that heroic figure guided by the classics rather than by Christian traditions and institutions, belongs as much to Alberti as to Nietzsche. Alberti, however, does not proclaim a dichotomy in traditional values; he recognizes only a conflict between true wisdom and the shrewdness that is a betrayal of moral principles. His treatise articulates an ethos and heroic ideals that would remain alive for the European intelligentsia for centuries. The idea of unselfish devotion to a humane wisdom survived both Machiavelli and Nietzsche in their different times and circumstances. It remains for many a moral obligation of intelligence to serve honorably the ungrateful masses and their no less ungrateful masters.

Before we consider the specific biographical and historical context of the work and explore some of the problems in Alberti's way of thinking, it may be useful to outline Alberti's argument.

Alberti introduces his subject by dedicating his treatise and justifying his venture. He hopes that his family will be pleased and that his older colleagues will be generous rather than critical. Wanting to say something that has not been said before, he will express what he has learned from his own experience. The question to be answered is whether education and devotion to learning lead to any of three possible rewards: pleasure, wealth, and prestige. Each of the next three sections of the treatise is devoted to one of these worldly goals.

Pleasure includes travel, sensuous comforts, play, the arts, and erotic pursuits, all of which will ruin the scholar if he engages in them—or so Alberti tries to convince his reader. Scholarship is an unrelenting task-master, and society, in any case, will drive the scholar back into his study.

The discussion of wealth appropriately involves an accounting. Alberti sketches the continual domestic expenses of the scholar, which exhaust his family's fortune and far outweigh the fees he is likely to earn. Alberti also tries to calculate the statistics of success: how many among the population of students will reach financial independence? By a series of careful steps, he arrives at the answer: one in a thousand. Finally, in a pessimistic and ironic spirit, he discusses whether a man of scholarly attainments will be in a position to marry for money. To do so, he says, will be well-nigh impossible and, if done, a terrible mistake.

Alberti argues that money does not come to a *litteratus*, that is, to a man of scholarly interests and attainments. If he is rich, it will not be because of his literary sophistication. If he is popular and trusted, thus obtaining many professional commissions, it will not be for his idealistic pursuit of knowledge. To sell his knowledge means to degrade himself and it. If he is a lawyer, for example, he will exhaust himself in an inane and poorly paid devotion to other men's causes. This, says Alberti, is essentially slavery. If he is a doctor, he will be a poor man unless he sells his services to murderers. If he is a preacher, he will engage in all sorts of chicanery to satisfy a congregation incapable of rising above frivolous and selfish concerns. If, on the other hand, he stubbornly devotes himself to learning itself, to truth and wisdom and not to mere deftness in the use of rhetoric, he will probably exhaust himself, live under wretched conditions, and die young.

Alberti makes an implicit distinction between the fame of learned writers and their position in public affairs. *Laus, gloria, nomen* (praise, glory, reputation) are words that Alberti uses for the public esteem that the man of letters strives and should strive to attain. In this connection, he talks about the pernicious effect of backbiters, slanderers, and malicious critics, who, he says, are quite common in the real world. His remarks suggest the importance, in his world, of reputation—of personal honor as dependent on how one is seen. It seems that this was a concern, not only for humanists, but for anyone who was ambitious in the close-knit, highly competitive society of Renaissance Florence. Turning to the issue of prestige in a more specific and practical sense, that is, to one's public status, position, and power, he believes that truly learned men preeminently deserve *auctoritas* and *honores* (civic authority and public recognition), but they do not get it, at least not unless they desert their books for administrative tasks. He demonstrates how humble will be their actual role in matters of state, even if they sacrifice time and energy to take part in such things, by describing the contempt in which such men are held by both the plutocrats who really run the city and the relatively powerless citizens who run after them. The implied context here, we note, is the republic of Florence.

In his concluding paragraphs, Alberti praises those who devote themselves to study, even though they will have to endure asceticism, poverty, and humiliation. The whole rhetorical exercise (which is by no means nothing but a rhetorical exercise) thus ends in a statement of quasi-religious devotion to secular learning.

The place of this treatise in Alberti's own life gives us a sense of its personal meaning. In the *Vita anonyma*, his autobiography of about 1441, Alberti writes that, from early youth on, he loved letters so much that "they seemed like flowering and fragrant blossoms," yet at other times they would seem to be "piling up under his eyes, looking like scorpions..."[3] It sounds like the actual letters on the page became unreadable to his over-strained eyes, but both the *Vita* and the much earlier *Use of Books* suggest there were psychological factors that sometimes made the very letters he was reading, copying, or writing turn into swarming poisonous insects. He claims that from childhood on, he pursued every art that he knew might bring a man glory. "As he grew into maturity, he put all other things second and dedicated himself wholly to the study of letters. He devoted some years to canon and to civil law..."[4] until he broke down, first at nineteen, then again at twenty-four, because of overwork as well as material deprivation. In *Use of Books*, he bases some of the troubles he says come with being a student on this repeated experience of physical and mental collapse. According to the *Vita*, at times when the letters began to writhe, Alberti would turn to music and painting and physical exercise.

Even in childhood, he says, bookish children are wan and anxious and are not liked by their peers. This raises a question: was the young Battista Alberti, before his university days, although, as the *Vita* claims, a versatile athlete and musician, somehow also like the scholar in *Use of Books*, a closeted over-studious boy whom others did not like? Alberti's friend and admirer, Lapo da Castiglioncho, who knew him from the age of fourteen, mentions that even as a child Alberti had spontaneously disdained children's games.[5] It is plausible that, though by no means exclusively interested in books, he was self-disciplined, serious, and critical beyond his years, and therefore did experience a kind of unpopularity.

Perhaps this history helps us understand the complaint in *Use of Books* that anything considered frivolous is out of bounds for a scholar, though everybody else is permitted to enjoy it. The ban on frivolity applies, not only because of other people's hostility, but also because the serious student cannot let go for a moment of his longing to achieve intellectual excellence and of the anxiety that attends ambition. The scholar in *Use of Books*, we realize, does not choose his ascetic way of life with the enthusiasm of Saint Francis marrying Lady Poverty. He suffers, and does not enjoy suffering. Yet he cannot escape his deprivation and loneliness without ruining his chance of greatness.

Alberti at nineteen, when he first became ill from too much study, wrote a Latin play, which he circulated anonymously and which was thought to be the recovered work of an ancient Roman. The play itself, *Philodoxeos*, is an allegorical drama in which the lover of truth is much mistreated by more worldly persons. Here and in some of the dramatic skits, the *Intercoenales*, written a few years later, Alberti expresses the pain of hostile exclusion. Alberti never mentions his illegitimacy, but this, and his growing up in exile in Genoa, Padua, and Venice, as well as the loss of his father when he was seventeen and the predatory behavior of certain family members thereafter (possibly in the scramble over inherited wealth) may have led to an uncomfortable reticence and inhibition in the company of other men. He lived—as no doubt many humanists did—with a very evident belief that the world was dangerous and envious of him, and with a dominant mood of highly focused determination. By the time he was writing *Use of Books*, he had probably visited Florence and come to know Brunelleschi and his circle.[6] There, practical jokes and light conversation (along with creativity and competition) were the norm, and Alberti the serious thinker (who was also, irrepressibly, an artist) may have felt the contrast sharply.

After his first breakdown in Bologna at nineteen, he returned to his (legal) studies, as he tells us, but became ill a second time at twenty-four: ". . . and finally he was stricken with a terrible affliction. As he was reading, the keenness of his eyesight suddenly failed, and he was overcome with dizziness and pain while a roaring and loud ringing filled his ears."[7] He also, as he tells us, lost his memory for names, though his visual memory was unimpaired. This time he did have to give up his studies of law "just as they were about to bear fruit."[8] Mancini, Alberti's first biographer, asserts on the basis of this phrase, and all subsequent scholars seem to agree, that Alberti did get a degree in law but then was unable to establish a practice.[9] It seems to me from Alberti's phrasing that he stopped just short of getting the degree. In either case, his breakdown at the age of twenty-four seems indicative, not only of overwork, but also of a profound revulsion from the study of legal texts, indeed of any texts. Isn't this suggested by the words of the *Vita*, that at this point he turned to mathematics and physics because he realized that these "exercised intelligence rather than memory?"[10] Did illness end Alberti's literary career then? Obviously not. He dealt with his desperate situation, he says, as well as with his ambivalence about literary work by writing.

"At this time he wrote for his brother the little book, *On the Advantages and Disadvantages of Letters*, where he set forth on the basis of experience what one should think of these studies. . . ."[11]

The treatise itself begins by referring to family members who helped Alberti and who expected something from him, some fruit of his studies. These persons in his family, the treatise suggests, were sympathetic to Alberti's love of literature but disturbed by his inability to support himself. Apparently some had pleaded with him to abandon his unprofitable concentration on literature and join the family business. In the treatise, Battista makes explicit how his values differ from those of a man of business. He also gives reasons for despairing of making a living as a classical scholar, a lawyer, a notary, or a scribe, without a powerful patron. He defends the study of books, that is, of truth, as the highest vocation. Thus, implicitly, he explains his choice not to return to Florence and not to join the family business. He explains, indirectly, why he is willing to lead a life dependent on patronage, for in fact, he is on the point of joining, or has joined, the household of Cardinal Albergati.

This step connected him with the papal court, and a few years later he became an apostolic secretary, part of the papal chancery. Entering on this career would involve ordination, either immediate or prospective, as a precondition for receiving income from prebends. The picture seems to be that in 1428, just as the ban on the Alberti family was being lifted in Florence, Battista's older brother Carlo moved there, found employment in the family's traditional banking business, and perhaps acquired wife, house, and children, while Battista joined the "family" of a cardinal, got ready to travel with him outside Italy, and committed himself to celibacy.[12] If the treatise, dedicated to Carlo, is a kind of rationalization of this situation, it becomes clear why the author so fervently attacks sex and love as inimical to the pursuit of learning, and marriage as thoroughly problematic for anyone who lacks financial independence. We can also understand why Battista argues at length that the professions, practiced independently as he himself might have practiced law or the notarial profession or even the priesthood in Florence, are either miserably paid or thoroughly corrupt. In *Use of Books* he writes as one who knows Florence and admires the republic for its freedom, yet has been disgusted by Florentine contempt for those who know and care about words and language.

The dedication to Carlo seems intended to lessen the social gap between Battista and his brother. Though Battista moved from the university to service in the church, and from Bologna to a life centered on Rome, he by no means wanted to forget Florence and be forgotten there, forget the Albertis or be forgotten by them. A few years later, he would write the first three books of *Della Famiglia*, celebrating the Alberti clan and writing in Tuscan for the Florentine republic. He would dedicate this work to his cousin Francesco Alberti, a fellow secretary in the papal chancery. In it, he would emphasize—though not without a touch of sarcasm at the expense of both sides—that men who had studied the classics held much basic wisdom in common with experienced but not classically educated businessmen, like the patriarchal old Gianozzo Alberti. There is more of a bitter division in *Use of Books*.

The author presents himself as a hurt and disillusioned young man. He suffered poverty, exhaustion, and illness and was blamed for his choice of life by members of his family. He had failed to become a practicing canon lawyer and legal scholar. Despite literary achievements, he could not survive on his reputation as writer unless he took up a humble post as teacher with some noble family. Instead, he gained a position in Cardinal Albergati's household; the cardinal was known to favor scholarship as well as a restrained, morally irreproachable way of life. But this would not bring Alberti a peaceful little house to write in: in fact, with Albergati he soon traveled to France, Germany, and the Low Countries. Writing before or after the fact in *Use of Books*, he comments that travel, although in the broad sense educational, is incompatible with the cultivation of learning. How will he manage to take or find books while traveling?

The social niche of bookish cleric and courtier in the church obviously did not please the young Alberti, and it seems he could not foresee how, without abandoning his passion for reading and writing, he would be able to burst out of the confines of a such a life. Indeed, when Alberti describes how unpopular a scholar is at a dance or as a suitor, how he is ridiculed by everybody when he dances or sings, he may be chafing—among other things—at the cassock he is wearing. In the course of years, however, his church position proved, not only a way to keep on with his study and writing, but a way to be an elegant diplomat and to some extent an influential critic of society. It allowed him to gain a high place in a society of his own. As Lapo da Castglioncho indicates in his dialogue of 1438 on the "Advantages and Disadvantages of the Papal Court," Alberti became, not a mere cleric and scribe, but a distinguished citizen at the capital of a glorious, if purely spiritual community—not the church, primarily, but "the republic of letters."[13]

In *Use of Books* Alberti laments, among other things, the common, too narrow view of what a scholar, writer, and thinker should do and not do. At moments he seems to join in with that view himself, when he describes how easy it is to lose one's erudition through interrupting one's work and how difficult it is to regain it. But he wanted, as he tells us, to excel in *everything* (bookish and otherwise) that could bring glory. Some ten years later, in the *Vita*, cloaked in anonymity, he describes his versatility with pride. What made the difference between the gloom in *Use of Books* and the self-assurance in the *Vita*? The "Renaissance man," whom the general public appears to have viewed with suspicion as he crossed professional and class lines, came into flower, nonetheless, under the system of patronage. Multifarious services could endear a courtier to his patron. Alberti's architectural career (for us his greatest claim to fame) was, according to Franco Borsi, a form of unpaid service to the pope, conciliating various problematic republics and princes.[14] Some of his architectural thinking was done in direct service to Pius II and to Nicolas V. The church thus became the best platform for Alberti, both as man of classical learning and as an artist. And no one had a more distinguished career as a courtier. Such a career is just what, in *Use of Books*, he claims is impossible for the serious scholar and what, therefore, he renounces.

Though it is rooted in the specific dilemma of Alberti in his twenties, *Use of Books* expresses ideas that have a wider base in the life of his time than his personal disappointments and choices.

Higher education as Alberti knew it began as young as twelve and continued through one's twenties, after which there was the problem of establishing one's reputation sufficiently to gain a professional position or practice. First one studied the trivium, that is, grammar, rhetoric, and dialectic (the term used by educators for philosophy); then one moved on to law, theology, or medicine. While the trivium was seen as preparation, it also had a life of its own, and in the period of developing humanism, it became much more important than before. While a humanist began with the traditional subject matter of rhetoric, he cultivated a wider range of Latin and, in Alberti's generation, Greek erudition. In doing this he depended on bought or borrowed manuscripts and on the advice of friends as he puzzled out unfamiliar material without the help of dictionaries or, in many cases, prior translations. Years, indeed decades, were spent developing one's knowledge of classical languages, mythology, history, and philosophy. To do so was difficult, but it seemed to the humanists that one could acquire wisdom, style, elegance, and character as well as the skill to pass these on. Classical authors were esteemed as by far the best teachers of the most important truths.

Humanism required a penchant for thinking in pre-Christian terms and generally inspired at least some degree of neopaganism. For men like Alberti, it was certainly not a matter of mere whim or reactive rebellion but was meant seriously to reform education and purify ethics. Literature, therefore, took on some of the dignity of a religion. A practical education might be the preference of most parents, a profound cultivation of theology or law the preference of most educators, but humanists believed in the ancient writers. According to Alberti, their wisdom (centered on Ciceronian Stoicism) would lift the student above worship of money and success and give his life meaning. "Books" taught one to despise venality and to reject many customs of the university, the church, and the contemporary political world.

On the material level, study was difficult indeed. Books were parchment and leather, and every copy was written by hand. What long hours, what vigils in cold rooms by candle light, were involved in the laborious reading and writing of texts. If one was poor, moreover, as students usually were, a warm coat and a box of coals under one's feet were unobtainable luxuries. One was chronically exposed to special physical discomfort and prone to illness, as well as threatened by the dangers that threatened others, the ever recurring onslaughts of war and plague. Unlike most of the poor, moreover, one was likely to be personally involved, through one's teachers and patrons, in the upheavals of city politics.

The labor of copying that was intrinsic to study had a particular intellectual effect: it made inevitable for all humanists the close association of calligraphy, the alphabet, language, and literature. Alberti went particularly far in recognizing these connections. He analyzed codes based on letters and numbers, and he wrote the first grammar of Italian. Unusually for his generation, he defended the use of the Italian language in serious literature. He argued that Latin itself had once been a spoken language, something most contemporary humanists did not believe. Writing made Latin last beyond its lifespan as a vernacular, Alberti implied, and writing can bestow similar dignity on Italian.

Although humanism involved a considerable amount of copying, memorizing, and quoting, Alberti, like Petrarch but unlike many of his own generation of humanists, always stressed originality in the handling of the classical vocabulary; anything he wrote had to be "something new."[15] He felt he had to add to what was known and understood, hard as that was to do and even though society as a whole neither cared nor helped. Perhaps like crafts today, humanism, as Alberti represented it, gave hope of reviving the venerated past by a judicious mixture of imitation and innovation. Like today's crafts, it was expensive but beautiful and dependent on the patronage of the wealthy. That humanism in education would become the wave of the future was both obvious and questionable. The humanists of Alberti's day self-consciously clung to their worth and described each other or themselves as "men of divine genius." They no more expected to be forgotten than discoverers expect the world to forget their discoveries. At the same time, they did not expect or want a mass movement to follow. They educated exclusively the rich, the powerful, and the gifted. They wrote for their patrons and each other. A wider audience, however, was growing. In response to the increasing demand for books, within a few decades printing was not only invented but established as an industry.

Alberti knew that more and more people were interested in education, that they wanted to read, profess, and teach. He argued in favor of providing them with a good vernacular literature. The flood of would-be classical scholars and professional men, however, he viewed as a degradation, an adulteration akin to the nouveau riche, as Dante described them, replacing old families in Florence.[16] Alberti saw the universities crowded with men "born to wield not the pen, but the spade, the ax, and the shepherd's crook." Rough hands have no business with manuscripts, rough minds are not awake to their meaning. Alberti scorned these poor newcomers as people who saw education as the key, not to inner development, but only to upward mobility. He especially, we can guess, did not want to be seen as one of them.

Upward mobility—which he did not condemn if it was obtained by honest economic pursuits—was not to be obtained by extended education but by effort and luck in war, in commerce, or even in farming. If we should see him as a "civic humanist," it must be because of this approval from on high of ordinary economic life. However, he was far from recommending that a man of learning take part; study of great books, according to Alberti, taught values at odds with economic striving. Education, if intended to bring upward mobility, was a perversion of itself, a waste of money, and a waste, also, of potentially useful workers. If you are poor and hoping to use your education for profit, you will not only fail but degrade the study of literature in the process. If you are born rich, on the other hand, or receive privileges for reasons that have nothing to do with education, you may wish to acquire education as an ornament, but the chances are that you will not take learning very seriously. The disinterested pursuit of truth, therefore, is the painful privilege of a self-selected few among the "well-born" and "free."

Certain tensions pervade the very structure of Alberti's argument. Alberti expressed his understanding of, on the one hand, a polarized moral universe and, on the other, an individual development process thanks to social and intellectual experience. Perhaps, for this reason, Alberti frequently argues that, first, a certain way of acting (for example, studying law to make money, or marrying for money) is wrong; second, it leads to unintended consequences; and third, it is hardly ever possible. His developmental understanding of the issues is clearest when he recounts, in specific instances, how people change in the course of life's stages and changing circumstances. He suggests that the way one lives, and even one's character, comes out of an accumulation of decisions made on the basis of insufficient information. He presents anecdotes that function as more than illustrations, indeed as evidence of how things are. He observes many an unwilled passage from innocent intention to diminished values.

While, on the one hand, he appears as a dispassionate observer and analyst, on the other hand, what a rhetoric of good and evil! Words for villainy, such as *turpus, crimen, rapini, flagitii*, and for true good, such as *probus, honestus*, and even *divinus*, seem to explode in the author's most heartfelt voice, as do cries of outrage and angry exclamations about the folly of objections. *Virtus* (virtue) is repeatedly used with broad but always moral connotation and refers to a metaphysical entity: "Virtue stands out and excels, for there is a certain divine power joined to it and involved with it by which we rise above all vices and mistaken ways, a power which brings and maintains praise, honor, a whole and lasting happiness, and peace of mind."[17] Man's special gift, that raises him above the animals, says Alberti, and makes him like God, is reason, the chief use of which is to discriminate between good and evil and to choose the former.

Yet, there is from the beginning, the other way of thinking about human opinions and choices. We learn that the author himself used to think differently than he does now, that he wandered into the field of philosophical and literary research with an innocent belief that the life of a scholar was happy in its general tone and rewarded by the public. He did not believe the lamentations he heard from scholars and blamed them for complaining or for sticking with that life if they did not like it. Now he has learned what sacrifices, not only material but also psychological, are involved in a life devoted to books. As the treatise moves on to present various positions on the subject of scholarship and the usefulness of the scholar, we see empathy with all positions. Alberti gives expression to the anguished choices forced on the scholar himself as he grows older. He claims to know specific persons who deny the value of scholarly pursuits and presents their views with a certain amount of irony, I think, but also with fairness. In other instances of regret or even dispraise, he brings forward vaguely described or even hypothetical speakers who, it is clear, represent closely what he has heard. (Some of them can still be heard saying "if you're so smart, why ain't you rich?") The vivid voices of Alberti's personages suggest individual character rooted in class interest.

In a sense this is true even of a personification of *litterae*, or books, as a collective entity, that twice addresses the poor scholar in a harshly demanding, possibly parental, way. First, the scholar's library demands more money for expansion. Money spent on personal pleasures, the books say, is stolen from *us*. At the end of the treatise, the books sum things up. We won't help you gain worldly advantages, they say frankly, but we are proud and demanding because we are the key to the highest good. As they speak, they seem to represent three levels of activity, being at once a medium of expression, a living guide, and a specific philosophical training.

The entire work, despite the coherent thesis at its center, is composed of dramatic—hence somewhat ambiguous—encounters. It conveys a mood of driving and striving, of anger and faith, yet is written in language that is often ironic, in arguments that exhibit and do not resolve conflict. It seems that Alberti believes crucial choices must be made, and he writes to influence people to make the right choices, to change their ways; yet he also perceives overwhelming realities inexorably shaping men and knowledge. He even in one instance shows unconscious forces at work in the way people look upon lawyers:

> The crowd, unable itself to beat the cunning bent on conquest and pillage with which their masters enter into lawsuits, when they see schemer colliding with schemer, glorify the winning schemer. Thus if an unscrupulous learned legalist takes up an unjust case, they will call him a great master, the best of men, and a great friend. They have come to think deception a virtue, they admire the art of creating a mask and a false image as a remarkable mobilization of knowledge, and they believe that malice and wickedness and deliberate misinformation are obtained from recondite knowledge. (see p. 36)

Here, perhaps, is the reason for the sense of suffering that imbues the treatise. The world is a place of cruelty, venality, corruption, enslavement, and death. The ideal world is one where none of this will hold true. Thought does not so much mediate between these worlds as roam over the human comedy finding numerous flawed answers and return to the realm of angels to weep. There is a great deal of empathy in what I have termed Alberti's developmental thinking, but every example leads back to absolute moral judgments. It seems to me Alberti's passion for and against social reality is what makes this treatise transcend its time.

Another problem or contradiction also makes it more than historically interesting. Though Alberti claims that the use of books as a way of personal advantage is both wrong and impossible, he reflects by what he shows us, and exemplifies by what he is, the very opposite. We see that most people did find compromises between the ideal and reality and that education was almost universally sought with hopes of gaining a good position in the world. Thus, the underlying message of the work may be considered consciously or unconsciously to contradict its proclaimed message. At the same time, and unambiguously, Alberti is mourning the spiritual poverty of a field that is meant to be the home of the spirit. This is the universal problem, which he conveys with his complicated play of voices, the clashing of passions. This problem troubles us when he hymns the ideal of humanism in his last sentence (see p. 54): "[W]e, like our forefathers, are roused and uplifted by the exhortation and admonishment of the written word to pursue our studies in such a way as to prove our virtue to all and allow no one to doubt that our striving is for wisdom alone."

Even when humanism became the basis for noble education all over Europe, when it turned into the basis of education for the ruling class, when it became entwined with a rationalist rather than pagan or platonic worldview, and when it eventually became linked to liberalism or conservatism in certain set ways, it continued to carry some of the significance Alberti gives it. Even today it implies, for the leading thinkers about the social purpose of education, heroic figures of individual intelligence who confront and verbally challenge a world of hustlers, bigots, and brutes. Humanism implies a faith in some kind of spiritual goal for individual intellectual activity and is, in its own way, as demanding as the faith of the Christian martyrs. This ideal kept Alberti in the state of unceasing anxiety he so vividly describes. Study was a form of fanatical devotion, harmful to his health but inspiring. Longing for wisdom to be acquired from the written word has also inspired people of the ensuing centuries and, I believe, similarly exhausts and inspires many today. Many in the intellectual elite, whether they defend literacy as a skill threatened by new technologies, or defend these technologies as a means to cultural renewal, long for truth and feel that education is corrupted by commercial interests.

The Use and Abuse of Books

I.

Our parent Lorenzo was, in his day, easily the wisest of all the Alberti clan, among other things, in the way he raised his children, and as you remember, Carlo, he reminded us never to be idle, in public or in private, and never to seem so.[18] We were brought up in line with our father's excellent ideas and in a manner proper to free men. In accordance with his teaching, you have always been active, both in business and in continued reading, while I, who dedicated myself to scholarship and put it above everything else, would give up any activity rather than let a day pass without reading or writing. Thanks to our upbringing, I am happy to say, that guided by the great writers, we bore with unperturbed spirit certain evils that long afflicted us and prudently avoided others. Our education, however, was worth our hard work not just because it benefited us personally but more importantly, I think, because it may allow us to meet the high expectations of our friends. Over time, those who have always cared about my honor and reputation have been increasingly eager to see some results from the long hours at my desk, to judge my progress by the fruit of my hard work and studious zeal.

For my own sake and my people's, therefore, I have meditated and thought long and hard, searching with all my ingenuity for a subject I could treat adequately and which would prove the quality of my intellect, so as to satisfy them if it lay within me. But nothing came to mind that had not been beautifully dealt with by the divinely inspired classical authors, so that no one of our time, however learned, could deal with it better than they, nor did there seem to be some topic left of the kind they had treated, that I could handle well and with grace. The ancients had encompassed all serious and comic material, leaving to us only the opportunity to read them and the obligation to admire. Older contemporaries of ours have seized on a few subjects that lay hidden, perhaps overlooked by the ancients, and have thus gained honor and fame. If one wants glory, however, one must be willing to write something that is not perfect and ideal rather than allow oneself to grow old in erudite silence. What to do? Would it be good enough to imitate Isocrates, the rhetorician said to have produced splendid orations praising Busiris, a horrible tyrant, and condemning Socrates, the best and most venerable philosopher?

I do believe that many things are permitted to the young for the sake of mental exercise, though they would not be proper for mature scholars. These, indeed, have traced the character of princes and the deeds of republics as well as the outcome of wars; we younger people, if at least we offer something new, ought not to have to worry about severe and, so to speak, excessive criticism from those who listen like mutes or little children with hearing too sensitive to sounds to distinguish meaning, as if a learned man need only have discriminating ears without bothering to understand. We cannot hope, by great application to study, to attain the glory of ancient eloquence and elegance; even if we tried for a long time with all our powers, we could attain only mediocre success. We should nonetheless maintain our habit of intellectual exercise, not expecting to please critics who have spent their lives learning only that nothing is worth their praise, but hoping to satisfy my own family and friends.[19] By this gift, may we win their greater acceptance and love. If beyond that, our work is not wholly rejected by scholars, we shall consider ourselves well received.

Following our custom and obeying the requests of my family, therefore, I have put forth this little treatise on the use and abuse of books. I thought it would please you, my brother, both because I have acted courteously toward my people and because, in this instance, I have hit on a topic that is neither commonplace nor already generally understood. The results of devotion to books I know from personal experience, having practiced it at every period of my life to the present. I earnestly beg you, my brother (if I may borrow your own phrasing in *Ephebis*) to read this little book of ours, correct it according to your own unswerving judgment, and by your emendations kindly make it better and more beautiful.

II.

I have often heard distinguished scholars say things about scholarship that could really make anyone give up the desire to engage in it. Among other points, for there were many and varied arguments, they were open about the fact that they themselves, though at one time they had chosen to study books, would, if they could start over, gladly take up any other kind of life. I was far from believing that they were sincere, these men who had never spent any period of their lives not engaged in the study of texts, and not only did I believe that they spoke quite differently from what they felt, but I actually blamed them a little for it. I thought it wrong for learned men to discourage younger students and also wrong for highly intelligent men to continue on a course if they did not really believe in it. I diligently interrogated many men of learning and discovered that in fact almost all were of the same mind, namely estranged from the very study of books to which they had devoted their lives. Yet, for some reason I remained unconvinced, despite their authority and arguments.

While they pronounced that there were many disadvantages to a life of study, I considered it the most joyful of vocations; while they thought the cultivation of knowledge preserved in books should rank lowest among all disciplines, I thought that it ought to be considered the highest. I dedicated myself completely to scholarship, omitting no aspect of generally admired learning, striving to master all subjects by hard work, meticulous care, and long hours, applying myself with the utmost zeal and scrupulous care. I could not imagine a higher value or purpose; I thought it the duty of a lofty soul to take on strenuous labors and tolerate hardship, long hours, and all the other cares and difficulties that accompany study, both for the sake of knowledge itself and in hope of honor and fame, which I believed could come to me through erudition. I adhered to this opinion and this goal, a very worthy way of thinking but not very realistic, as long as I remained ignorant of what the ways of the world actually demand of us.

When, by repeated experience and by having to deal with society, I finally came to see the prevailing situation more clearly, I must confess that some of those arguments concerning the disadvantages of a scholar's life, which I was accustomed to reject, despise, and oppose in public, began to convince me inwardly, for I realized that they were indeed to a great extent true: the life of those who devoted themselves to books was actually more arduous and more unavoidably troubling than any other, and any other was far more likely to be easy and fortunate. Eventually I could hardly understand what serious students were hoping to accomplish with such strenuous effort and such an outpouring of energy, unless perhaps they derived from books some wisdom which enabled them to bear hardships that would have broken anyone else. I am, in fact, convinced that I myself, because of my years of study, lost my health and broke down from overwork, besides being robbed of all my worldly goods. But of my misfortunes elsewhere.[20]

Let this suffice for now to indicate why I do not altogether despise the feelings of those who, as they reported, would prefer to have spent their lives doing anything rather than reading. Yet, having discovered that the study of books is not, as I used to think, the way to personal advantage, I have not swerved so far from my old position as to think scholarship should simply be abandoned. I now believe that the study of books must be based on the conviction that, compared to knowledge of the loftiest matters, the goods of fortune hardly matter and that we will be content with wisdom alone. If I here present my views on the life of learning, it will not, I think, bore you or waste your time. For you will see that it is a mistake to promise yourself something from these studies other than a free and unprejudiced understanding. You will also be able to judge for yourself the utter folly of those who plunge into the immense labors required by scholarship because they want wealth, social recognition, or similar vain and transitory rewards.

For the life men of learning live is necessarily hard and harsh; by this I mean the ones who, as they should, abandon all other things for the sake of intellectual work. No art, however minor, demands less than total dedication if you want to excel in it. What we know to be true of all other arts is most especially true of reading and writing; there is no freedom from striving at any age. We see those who dedicate themselves to study poring over books, as the expression goes, from an early age, and left alone by everybody; we see them worn out and exhausted by anxious worrying—about the rod, the teachers, the struggle to learn—and by their constant assiduous reading. They often look anemic and lethargic for their age. In the next period, youth, when we are told that we can expect to see joy and happiness in boys' faces, look at their pallor, their melancholy, how in every aspect of their physical bearing, as they come out of their daily imprisonment in schools and libraries, they seem repressed and almost crushed. Poor creatures, how exhausted, how listless they are, thanks to long hours of wearisome reading, lack of sleep, too much mental effort, too many deep concerns. Anyone with a bit of humanity in him tends to pity their relentless toil or angrily condemn their folly, especially if they have hopes of being eventually rewarded by fortune. And rightly so, for outside of knowledge itself, no success (as measured by fortune's goods) is going to come their way. They are very mistaken if they waste their labor and ambition on this particular pursuit, while a life led along other lines could, with no more labor and striving, probably raise them to the highest pinnacle of financial and social success.

For the primary transitory goods that mortals value are: wealth for some, public recognition for others, and for still others, pleasure. Each of these is the object of intense competition. What else one may expect to gain from fortune I don't know; I believe there is nothing else fortune can bestow on us that anyone could want. From these prizes, however, scholars are excluded. To make this perfectly clear, I shall show first how much they get to enjoy themselves, second what fortunes fall in their laps, and finally, what honors are likely to be showered upon them. Our whole discourse will be succinct and brief considering the size of the subject, since its purpose is not to puff up with rhetoric but simply to set forth the facts concerning the advantages and disadvantages of study and, in view of these, to give good advice as to the right way to act. I shall omit many turns of speech that might move you and many kinds of argument, for I do not want even to appear to be trying to mock the disciplines or to be eager to expose learning to scorn. For those who expect something from reading and study besides erudition and wisdom, it will be useful, I think, to learn how things really are, to follow our argument and consequently turn away from their mistaken path. To frugal and prudent students, on the other hand, it will be a valuable reminder that books can give them true guidance and a real understanding of things, while all the rest is not worth thinking about. So let us now proceed.

III.

First, here is my opinion: anyone who is poor lacks the means, or at least the best way, to procure pleasures (that is, money) and, therefore, cannot fulfill the requirements of any discipline with much pleasure. For if pleasure is, as they say, that which moves the senses and delights the heart with a certain happy feeling,[21] and if all the things by which the senses are pleased, such as good things to eat or fine ointments and other luxuries, are unobtainable without money, how then, will a poor man be able to keep himself supplied with them? And how can he be happy when his poverty makes him incline to grief rather than delight?

It is obvious that luxuries belong by nature to the rich and the leisured: they are the ones who can pursue and collect diverse beautiful things. In my experience, however, you won't find many rich men who think books, let alone the delights of study, are worth the effort. Too many other pleasures beckon the wealthy from all sides, so that they are more likely to want to pursue familiar pleasures among friends than to join us in exploring unfamiliar texts. If by chance they do become interested in these, we wonder whether they will be as successful in this as they hope. It is abundantly clear if one considers the matter from all sides, that what we have already spoken of is true: the life of the studious is by its very nature burdened with many serious difficulties. From childhood on through every age, as we have seen, they are pressured and loaded with work, and scholars' nights as well as days are never free of anxiety and striving, so that it is implausible that they will find much there that smacks of even a little pleasure.

One of the greatest pleasures, for instance, and one worthy of a free man, is to wander through cities and regions: to gaze upon temples, theaters, fortifications and all sorts of buildings, to walk in places which, by nature and by human labor and design, have been made beautiful, welcoming, and secure. Serious students, however, are quite deprived, are they not, of such delights? It is hard to take along a lot of books while traveling, nor does one find much time to read when sightseeing. Of course, nothing will hold you back from roaming with great enjoyment through the provinces if you think you can be a learned man without reading much or often!

Beware, however, for it may be that travel is not only inconvenient to the pursuit of learning but ought to be viewed by scholars as more dangerous for other reasons: in particular, because such scholars, even if they stay in their own country, incur much disapproval for taking part in small pleasures that do not even amount to major distractions. To take just a few examples, who does not see at weddings, concerts, singing groups, or young people's games how scholars are looked on with scorn and even hatred? Everybody thinks it becoming in a young man to play the lyre, to dance, and generally to practice the pleasing arts, and people consider these appropriate activities for the young. Those who are even moderately skilled in such arts are generally welcomed and are popular. If they are credited with some such ability, they are invited and asked to join in. But not the young scholars, *they* are pushed away and excluded. If they show their wan faces at such occasions, people consider them either ridiculous or burdensome, and if they try to participate, how they are laughed at and what disparaging remarks they get to hear! Who doesn't look down on a singing or dancing scholar? They'll soon find that they are seen as mimes and actors of the silliest sort, and with the awareness, if they are men of feeling, will come regret and pain. Thus, what brings others lightness of heart brings dejection to the scholar; what brings others praise brings them condemnation; what brings others invitations brings them an invitation to leave. So young men devoted to study are not unreasonable, in my opinion, if they foresee that they may not travel in other regions for pleasure, since even in their own country they are not allowed to take part without shame in agreeable and joyful gatherings. Thus, if they have thought of gaining any sort of fame or noble reputation, they will stay nicely shut up at home, renouncing elegant, pleasant, and admirable things and forbidding themselves all access to these in order, as their work requires, to dig most diligently through their books; indeed they will not permit themselves any pleasure in exploring external things that might distract their minds and disturb their concentration.

Next after these distractions, one thinks of the pleasures of love, which I wish the serious student to forego entirely; for wise men have taught us that these pleasures are by nature harmful to all, but they are much more evil and pernicious for the scholar. Who, with a mind occupied by love, will be able to focus whole and steadfast attention on texts? Who can then be fully absorbed in his work, intent on the teachings, ready and able to store up and retain them? Who, when captive to the madness of love, will have the will power and intellectual vigor and enthusiasm to perfect himself in any noble art? Don't we know how love usually affects people? Sapping energy, corrupting conduct, perverting the intelligence, loading the mind with obsessions, filling the intellect with errors, driving a man to madness: these are its well-known services, the gifts that it bestows. But I won't go into all aspects of such pleasures (lest I become too involved with them) nor discuss how much more difficult it is for scholars and writers than for other people to be successful in these pursuits, how great the contrast between the handsomeness of courtiers and the sad squalor of scholars. I won't go into the luxuries of dress, the leisure time a suitor must have, and all those kinds of requirements. Let us take all that as said. Everyone knows that in these things scholars and writers score very low.

I do want to make myself clear on one point: for serious students all pleasures are a bad idea and harmful. The customs associated with conviviality and with Venus first of all (as everyone knows) invite the mind to relax and neglect matters of duty; they turn it away from persistence in reading, without which, and an immense amount of it, a man is sadly mistaken if he thinks he will somehow be an outstanding scholar. I don't know what it is in study, but characteristically, the more you learn, the more you realize how much you do not know and feel that you should study more zealously. Meanwhile, the odors of food and wine, and those of Venus, cause the senses to empty the mind and fill it with shadows, to spatter the intellect with dirt, to dull the powers of perception, and to occupy the seat of memory with doubts and suspicions and with various amatory images that thoroughly perturb the spirit. So it is that the mind which is caught up in pleasures and set aflame by amatory appearances will be constantly agitated, looking outward under the influence of an endless flux of unstable wishes and expectations. Who could be less apt and less skillful as a practitioner of the advanced disciplines and noble arts than a man thus love-struck in spirit and mind?

Scholars, therefore, will receive no pleasure, or very little, from food and from Venus, they will have minimal periods of sleep and rest and allow themselves only rare and carefully rationed participation in games and festivities. They will always act as if restrained by a law that belongs to their kind of work, a law that makes it impossible to depart without shame from their eternal meditations and ever-present intellectual concerns. For they know that, unless they work consistently, even the hardest and most intense efforts in the field of letters will be wasted. A brief period away from study has the power to disperse more material than many long hours of application can restore; things placed in memory slip away faster than they can be rememorized or recaptured. The various kinds of sensual pleasure, if permitted to scholars in small amounts, must be pursued in a very restricted measure and, if extremely harmful, must be assiduously avoided. One cannot honestly say that serious students can somehow indulge in recreation without loss of dignity or linger in pursuit of diversion without undermining their work.

Can a man enjoy refreshment of spirit, in any case, when he is not unmindful that great expectations are fixed on him and that, if he does a mediocre job of meeting them, he will be disgraced more than any poor wretch? Will he really act with carefree and unburdened spirit if he can look around and see that his relatives, friends, and acquaintances all desire and expect some great achievement from him? And on top of that, what if he is not unaware that there are rivals, back-biters, and destructive critics (not a terribly rare type of men) prepared to find fault and speak slanderously of him if, through negligence, or desire, or for the sake of pleasure, he does something that prevents his attaining to the highest level of intellectual competence? What will his thoughts be when he indulges in pleasure, he who was destined for an occupation full of labors and dangers that held the promise of greatness? Won't he be cruelly tormented all the time by worry, anxiety, and a certain fear of disapproval?

I think that he who knows these things, and understands that he must by hard study and relentless application meet family expectations, escape the efforts of envious men to bring him down, avoid damage to his reputation, and attain some sort of glory, will choose not to take up the many heavy and harsh burdens that await the studious rather than to embark on a scholarly career and then give it up. For this presents a terrible dilemma: to leave the hard, harsh, difficult field of letters with unavoidable disgrace or remain in it with extreme and relentless efforts and great hardship. Once having started, you will be afraid to turn to lighter things and abandon serious study without some immense good reason. You will be forced to choose which burden you can bear with less harm to your pride, the frank admission that your mind is not good enough for scholarly work or the implication that your spirit and character are too craven to stand up under the strain. There is a further problem: scholars, if they change their minds, being unpracticed and ignorant in all other arts, can discern nothing outside of books to which they can devote themselves with honor. What then? Is it gratifying to the scholar's heart to realize that, if he leaves his chosen pursuit of the loftiest knowledge, he is destined for an abject and almost shameful future and that, therefore, he must sweat perpetually in bitter and unceasing toil? What will shame you more deeply among your kin than not to be what you strove at every age to become? To show the world that you are not very learned, after all, precisely in the field you always cultivated to the exclusion of all else? To fail to shine in the field where you spent enough time to have attained excellence? Will it really be a trivial matter for him to withdraw at some point from the continuous labors of scholarship and let everyone see that he has slowed down or broken off from his chosen path to glory? Wretched the man who, for the sake of pleasure, runs right into the sword of critics and gossips.

Not least likely to be harmed by pleasure are those who discover belatedly that, because they dropped their work or even just took a vacation, they have wasted all their preceding years of labor. If a man realizes that this will happen, as indeed it will, how can he actually enjoy any recreation? When he happens to encounter some comfort or enjoyment, or some sweet pleasure, even as he reaches out for it, sharp anxiety about his honor will make him feel faint and fear of a desolating loss of reputation will terrify him. No whole-hearted joy or celebratory moment or happiness is possible for you, my scholarly friend, as long as you are always caught up in study, wrapped up and buried in manuscripts. No ecstatic pleasure and light-hearted soaring can seize you if you partly desire the huge burden of study and partly are afraid to put it down. I won't remind you here how great is the anxiety experienced by those who long for glory, who want to surpass all rivals or at least to be surpassed by none.

All this aside, the life of the studious man, unless I am mistaken, is by far the most painful life, especially if he has any longing for the things that a young man of generous disposition is naturally somewhat inclined to want. For if he wishes to turn his mind and hand to horsemanship and the training of dogs, or to athletic games, or to other activities proper to a free man, how sadly he will abandon all pursuits that bring dignity and honor to youth and, for very shame at his own lack of glory, shut himself up in libraries, permitting himself nothing, however fine and noble, but midnight oil and books! Not without great agony, believe me, do we abandon pursuits that others praise so much, knowing they would turn us away from study and bring down eventual scorn on our heads.

Indeed men who usually sit in judgment and censure all conduct, take a heavier line with scholars than they should or than they do with others: "What's he doing out at this time of day? It's not right." "These clothes are not appropriate for him." "We don't approve of the company he keeps." "This place is disreputable, he should not be there." "This is not proper conduct for a man in his position." "Those words he used are disgraceful." On and on. They are all watching the scholar with infinite dislike, looking for the chance to tear apart his reputation, so that, unless you want to be thought of as an irresponsible dandy and shady character, it's obvious that you have to live, not according to your own judgment and free will, but to suit the narrowest prejudices of the common people.

What happens if, by some chance, you decide to ignore public opinion? When you wish to buy clothes, isn't it true that your library will say to you: "You owe *me* that money, I forbid . . ." If you wish to pursue the hunt, or music, or the martial arts or sports, won't the books say: "You are stealing this energy from *us*, we will not bring you fame and reputation!" If you inquire into technical knowledge or painting or three dimensional design, the philosophical disciplines will react strongly: "This is the way you defraud *us* of your energies. From you we will withhold knowledge of the highest things. . . !"

If you want to refresh your spirit by a country excursion (I am not speaking of travel to distant places), the vocation you have taken up will pull you back from there to books and writing, and if you do not with much labor and long hours devote yourself totally to these, the books themselves will threaten you with shattering disgrace. Serious students must, in addition, deprive themselves of the pleasant consoling company of their fellow citizens, must enjoy solitude, must avoid all discourse except the kind flavored with scholarship and a certain elderly sobriety. To them the leisure to chat with friends, to walk around, to make new friends is simply forbidden. Some hours are given to reading, others to listening, and very few are left at their disposal. Almost no time remains for pursuing unalloyed pleasure. What a life of self-indulgence! To relax or slow down the labors that keep him in chains is plainly forbidden; he lives according to the hostile judgment of others; the resources of youth, the sweetness of the prime of life, the best years, and indeed all the years of his life must be entombed in piles of paper and dead sheep (as I may call books).[22] The scholar is as much confined as if serving a life sentence, and necessity pits him always against nature.

If, then, every pleasure serves to distract the scholar's mind from his work, if (as it seems) an infinite number of pleasurable pursuits are out of bounds as harmful to his vocation, if the scholar is required to renounce all these, what life that men lead is harder? If the scholar is never allowed to take time away from his studies to explore and observe, to enjoy himself, to extend the periods of sleep and leisure, or to pursue any personal advantage, if on the contrary, the moments that he does not owe to his books are few and far between, who can possibly dare to say that he is a man of books and learning for pleasure's sake?

But I would not want to obscure the true nature of scholars by concluding that they devote themselves to books with *no* idea of pleasure. They could not perform such great labors without some notion of pleasure in their minds. There are those who willingly go into mourning, because they take pleasure from being considered very faithful and true to the memory of friendship. Many actions by which we satisfy convention and public opinion seem less painful to us than they really are. The pleasure of study, however, is such that it might better be called pain: sedentary all the time, reading all the time, thinking hard, always alone, renouncing festivities and play. I am not so bitter and hard a man that I would dare call this a pleasant way to live. There is a special sort of pleasure in avenging injuries, in plotting and conspiracies, in assaults and battles that lead to your overcoming enemies by your own powers; still, hostile conspiracies and hatred are extremely painful. What happens in the pursuit of letters is similar. To satisfy the desire to learn is indeed a pleasure, but the very hard work of study and the accompanying anxiety that oppresses the spirit always bring more mental torment than joy. So if we indeed take a certain pleasure in learning, huge cares and labors undermine it. There is a big difference, moreover, between the burden of fighting the intrigues and assaults of enemies, which is experienced relatively briefly, and the scholar's daily anxiety, which is perpetual and immense. For there are innumerable things in books that are supremely worth knowing, nor is it easy to describe how the desire to learn presses upon a scholar. He may participate in difficult scholarly debates, or explore some elegant, worthy, and learned subject; while he does so, he does not sleep, does not eat, does not rest, and feels almost no satisfaction. The desire to know and to remember it all is constantly gnawing at him. He takes on immense projects, is entangled in an array of possible rhetorical devices, is constantly tense. On top of this, he is always coming across things previously unknown to him: he encounters in his reading adroit, subtle and clever ideas, finds some unusual illustrative anecdote, or learns new refinements of the power of persuasion; these things provoke in him the desire to learn more, and he is unable to set limits or stop, nor is he granted any peace of mind as long as he has not cleared up every obscurity. Thus, as you see, the scholar is a very complex puzzle himself, and neither physically nor mentally ever, or hardly ever, gets any rest. Bleak solitude, hard labor, endless hours, great anxiety, difficult questions, total absorption, intense anxiety—as there is no pleasure to be found in this man, so in his whole life there is almost no break in the onslaught of work and worry.

That's how things are, and therefore, I think this can be said of a scholarly life: no prudent person will be lured into it by hope of pleasure. But perhaps you think that the idea of acquiring wealth and power, or gaining honor and status, may be a reason for the learned to choose this life?

IV.

Since we said that after treating of pleasure, we would discuss wealth, let us now consider how the study of books leads to prosperity. I deny that wealth results from scholarly excellence. I do not deny that it is possible for someone to become moderately well-off who devotes himself conscientiously, as he should, to intellectual labors. I want it understood, however, that such labors do not enable even the most covetous and diligent practitioners to accumulate really great wealth. If I show that this is the truth, it will be perfectly clear how little wisdom there is in dedicating oneself to learning in the expectation of riches.

Why is it that, of the many men of learning whom we see in every region, we see so few whose wealth is impressive? I have myself been able to observe some among their number who were not poor, of whom I have been able to determine without insulting anyone, either that they were not extremely wealthy or that they had gained their wealth in other ways, not by their learning. If scholarly ability helped one to become wealthy, how is it that we do not find all men of learning equally fortunate? Why do we see many outstanding scholars in humble circumstances? Whence comes this discrepancy between scholars who labor in dire poverty and a single individual of better than mediocre intellectual attainments who rejoices in ample means? Shall we deny because of this one case that study does little to foster personal prosperity? We are more inclined to conclude that men of letters are all poor because, being occupied with study, they neglect all else, not only their health but even more their domestic affairs, and seem either unaccustomed or unable to take much interest in their finances.

There is another reason, it seems to me, why the learned are excluded from material success, for they acknowledge a different passion and a different ability rather than the passion for profit and the talent for making money. What they are taught by good books is modesty, magnanimity, virtue, and wisdom. With hope and zeal, they apply their talent to acquire these traits, which forbid concentration on the pursuit of money and on a multitude of other pursuits, for a rightly directed mind does not dwell among perishable things where wisdom and virtue are given a low priority. Men are praised for putting aside covetousness and training themselves to esteem, not the wealth which is denied to the man of learning, but the marvelous truths he can come to know.

Now one may well ask what ability and what steps do lead to wealth. It has been said that there are two ways for mortals to become rich: either by the help of fortune or by the application of knowledge. And this, I think, is correct. By fortune we may become rich through inheritance, some legacy, or gifts and largesse of the kind that come to us by chance, or, on the other hand, we may grow rich by our own doing, by industriousness, as in business or in paid services and the rewards thereof. Let us inquire whether study can take us on either path.

Since we set out to discuss the advantages and disadvantages of learning, perhaps it is not even appropriate to discuss the good or bad fortune that befalls learned men, since the opinion of all good authors is that fortune of whatever kind is to be borne and not to be thought about. For this reason, though we shall treat of these matters and not neglect whatever points are relevant, we shall be so brief that I may seem to have deliberately omitted more than I decided to include. I do not want to seem over-interested in these matters, lest I be accused of disrespect for scholars.

Now they say that wealth grows rapidly when money comes in thick and fast while expenses are moderate and infrequent—a neat formula. The household store increases when you add more each day than you take away. But it is just the other way with men of learning, since they receive meager payment and at every age spend lavishly. No wonder, then, that they are poor. If anyone doubts that the study of books involves great expenditures, I have a clear and relevant story to show, not only that vast sums are drained away by this pursuit, but also that it brings major and unending harm to the scholar's family.

I am thinking of something I heard in Bologna, where I was a student, from a certain honorable citizen, the father of a legal scholar, who told me more than once that there was nothing he regretted as much in his life as having let his son embark on these studies. He said it had led to much trouble, first because he felt that his son's knowledge was of no practical use, as he never wanted to distract the young man from his work to assist the family. His son, therefore, had come to count for him as one of the useless members of his household. If he had not chosen to have him pursue advanced legal studies, there were many things he might have taken care of which his father now had to pay others high fees to manage, fees that greatly reduced his profits. Things would have been very different if he could have used his son, and not outsiders, in his business. The returns would have been very little reduced by fees, nor would the family have been forced to waste money on various major expenses incurred by the son. Masters had to be paid, money given to grammarians, dialecticians, other teachers too, books purchased, then more books, and more books after that, so that there was no end to the bills of scribes and others. On top of this came those forms of ostentation associated with the achievement of the doctorate. How much was given away and dissipated, what big sums were demanded for clothes and university gowns, for a celebratory feast, even for remodeling the house and embellishing it, plus all kinds of additional craziness, until almost the whole fortune of the family was exhausted. If only there were some limit to this kind of thing, instead of expenditures growing from day to day, both at home and in public! Formerly he lived in the private, frugal, and honest style of his ancestors, but now, with the gown of the doctorate and the increased celebrity of his name, everything had to be more elegant and showy. The father could never hope to receive sufficient compensation for all this. To this he added another good point, well known to others no doubt, but new to me: "If the money lying idle in those books and clothes my son acquired had been invested in business, as it might have been, it would have grown into a fortune, and I would not only have kept what I spent on him but taken in additional income from year to year."

  The loving father often talked this way of the damage and loss he had suffered. He further declared that he was not so much troubled by his son's immoderate and wasteful expenses as grieved by the realization that he could not hope for much from the young man, whom relentless scholarly labors had turned into an invalid and who, as his father observed, would take no rest even in his weakened condition. The grief-stricken father would try, with parental solicitude, to offer his son some sort of play or diversion and would frequently order him not to mortify himself to such an extent with sleepless nights and fasting.

  But to these demands, the son regularly replied along the following lines: "Don't, my father, don't try to hold us back from our chosen path. You should realize that I have a duty to pursue my work with this kind of zeal; if you are wise, if you care for our dignity, urge me to keep more vigorously at my books, order me in the future never to leave the library at all. Beware, lest, by your direction, you may tend to undermine the reputation which our care and diligence has brought us. I would rather hear you ordering me, father, to uphold with all my will and strength the trust my clients repose in me and the causes of friends that I have taken up; for I am sure you can easily understand that it is to fulfill their expectations that I am thus defending my long hours. Therefore, father, let me carry on."

  This prudent citizen and father, in part because he was really afraid that this way of life was undermining his son's health, tried everything, though in vain, to get him to drop his studies. The loving father thought he would rather have a robust, happy, and healthy son, even if not so erudite, than one who was nervous, sad, anemic, and ill. Often he vowed he would rather have an ignorant son than a supremely learned one. For, he said, it is enough to have a son who causes no harm to his country and family. It was a truly great grief to him that this one had to be maintained at such cost.

This very unassuming man came to his view of things not because of some prejudice, but by experience, as he watched what the scholar was costing him. If an upright citizen is worthy of belief, and this man, among the most respected in his city, bore witness as I have reported with full agreement from his hearers, shouldn't he convince anyone that letters are not the road to wealth? Doesn't he offer excellent proof that preparation for a learned profession not only does not bring wealth but involves a sad and exhausting life of heavy burdens and labors, a life to be avoided?

And if even he, a father who had kept his son at home, felt this way, what will fathers say whose sons are living in distant cities, where none of the fruit of the family's land can be used to sustain them, where not the least thing can be had without cash, where physical needs and care of the body must all be paid for by draining the father's coffers? If clothing is needed, if they want books, if they are ill (which happens all the time), how much money is to be thrown into this bottomless pit? It is hard to describe how prodigal young men tend to be, far away from the intimidating presence of their elders, how freely they entertain and give presents to their comrades. If you calculate all that in, you will realize without a doubt that those who study spend far more money while they devote themselves to books than they will ever recoup by the practice of a scholarly profession. So? What sure and great gain is to be anticipated at the end, to justify first throwing away your entire fortune? A wonderful career, this, which first absorbs the father's goods and exhausts his inheritance from his ancestors, then offers only illusory hopes!

So we see what comes of study, what failure awaits those who try to make money out of scholarly training. It is known that a good income from any of the arts is acquired either as frequent small earnings or as earnings that are large though infrequent. Unless I am mistaken, no art earns sums that are at once great and frequent. Great rewards are earned by vast and unceasing labor producing highly specialized and original work. Such work is usually beyond the artist's capacity, and such rewards beyond the buyer's. What I want to establish here is that you, the student, should not hope to get rich from the meager fees you will earn for teaching a child, for writing a book, for pleading a case, for curing a fever, or for expounding a mass of things concerning law or whatever. Indeed, such earnings barely cover daily necessities. And they come at such long intervals that they can only allow you to accumulate savings slowly, arriving very late at wealth.

But men of letters are not *never* rich. I don't want to seem stubborn. I admit that some of them, sometimes, are not wretchedly poor. But if they are really wealthy, we think it is from some source other than their learning. Perhaps they illustrate the attainment of wealth by the exercise of avarice, crime and fraud, which dirty money they may try to cover up by the splendor of a reputation for learning. That, in my opinion, makes them doubly guilty: first because they aggrandize themselves through evil, and second because, with their vileness, they bring down the honor and dignity of letters. Is it inevitable, then, that honest men of learning will be poor? Indeed they will if they choose to abound in knowledge rather than cash, in character rather than precious metals, a richly furnished mind rather than a richly furnished home. What if they pursue both literature and wealth? They will hardly be equally outstanding in both. And why not? Because the passion of a man dedicated to knowledge is different from that of the man whose passion is for acquisition, and totally opposite. The one group spends time and energy on usury, theft, rapine, and crime. What could be more foul? The other seeks respect, praise, and the acclaim of posterity. What could be more beautiful? On one side we have those who prefer amassing gold to glory, wealth to fame, perishable material things to the gratitude and good will of their fellow citizens. On the other are those who hardly care to spend anything except to support solid and whole personal goodness. What men of learning and students of the noble arts scorn, acquisitive men pursue, while what scholarly men seek is of no interest to the acquisitive man. To attain their goal of aggrandizement, moreover, the covetous will make use of robbery and avarice, while men of learning, in enhancing their good name, take delight in liberality and justice. But to put an end to this discussion, here is my view: learned men will not become rich, or if they gain wealth by their learning, they do so wickedly. For no one whose spirit is not conniving preys on others (not to go into the other vile ways of the covetous). No one who is not degenerate chooses to put elegant learning second to moneymaking. No one who is not deeply corrupted will think of making learning a form of commerce for his own enrichment.

If, nonetheless, contrary to all tradition and ancient precedents, anyone should become justly rich for his learning, he clearly must be more at ease with fortune, more knowledgeable, more authoritative; his friendships must be greater, more numerous and more lasting than those of other men; his good nature, flair, intelligence, craftiness, and cleverness must be more suited than other men's to please all ears and accommodate all opinions. Such must this man of learning be, and while the city gladly entrusts him with the fortunes of all, he may display abundant wealth and frequent rewards. But truly men of such high reputation are rarely encountered, and, I must add, anyone who wishes to be favored by a great many people must exhibit, not avarice and the kind of skills that lead to accumulation of money, but kindness, liberality, and even prodigality, traits, as you know, not very helpful in gathering wealth.

Or let us hypothesize that there are many whom the whole city dares to trust, so that all jobs of litigation, of oration, of healing illnesses fall to them, I say that all these commissions taken together and given to just one learned man would not in my judgment (may the gods help me) be so lucrative and so numerous as to make that man truly wealthy. How many illnesses, or rather plagues would it take, how many quarrels would have to fill the civil courts, and what hunters of unusual opportunities to make money would we have to be, good gods, before we could earn a just wage by literary skill, before we would be able to live in an honorable way, not by the largesse of others but by our own earnings? Where does all this take us? Obviously, to the realization that not one scholar can ever, by his own meager earnings, become rich, or at least hardly one of the many who try.

Nor do I feel that we should listen to those who would bring up the saying: "If you don't cheat, you won't make money; if you don't catch it in a trap, you won't catch profit." For the art of making money is very different from the art and dignity of those who are learned, but there are numerous and sure ways, outside of scholarly activity, to make money by honest application to a variety of civil arts, too many, in fact, to list here. Let this be clearly understood: all other arts or skills will bring in money more easily than the study of books. If you choose a military career, for instance, it will often happen that you gain a great deal of wealth compared to the little you would gain from erudition. Where there are armed soldiers in the field many ways open up to gain riches, even to rise to the highest pinnacles of wealth. But if you want literary jobs that pay, you must be very humble and very mercenary. What if you are a businessman? Won't you make as much money as you want? Won't there be ports and regions and peoples everywhere who will look to you to bring them goods? Or if you practice agriculture? What way of life is more blessed? What more fruitful, profitable, and respected occupation could you find? Only agriculture can give comfort, peace, and freedom to the ignorant but can also make learned men happy. For no expectation of returns is surer than that given by a well-cultivated field, while at the same time the country provides leisure to live well and blessedly away from all noise and bother. In addition, there is nothing more valuable and perennially useful than what is gained by agriculture. But the praises of agriculture and other profitable arts will have to wait for another occasion. In all of them, and in all other arts and occupations, making money is in a certain sense logically part of the work. In scholarship, by contrast, the rewards that come naturally are elegance of thought and moral refinement, which prudent men generally consider the purpose of their study, so that it is more becoming to bear poverty with fortitude for the sake of knowledge than to gain wealth without honor.

In case there are any men so shameless that, in disregard of the sacred dignity and moral code of learning, they have let their greed convince them that, with fraud and deceit, they can make money by the choice of a scholarly career, I want them to know they are greatly mistaken. For there are an infinite number of possible accidents that in fact prevent all but a very few mortals from reaching the point where the first monetary rewards of study are available. Let us omit here the possibility that the father's fortune may be exhausted by the cost of studies before the student has reached the level of skill required to support himself by the sale of his learned services. It is very well known that the man who wishes to make money from academic knowledge cannot begin to sell anything until he has proved himself to have some extraordinary level of knowledge. Hence we see them showing off whatever brilliance and learning they possess in speeches, disputations and debates, at schools and gymnasia [universities] and public occasions. Nor is it permitted to go on from there to making money unless they get people to think that they are considered learned by the public. This, they believe, will lead more readily than actual merit to the earning of money. So they want to be called doctor and see men admire their gold clasp, which is the sort of thing they emphasize, as if with these symbols they have great knowledge, and without them have learned nothing.

Now it seems highly appropriate to ask whether they return home with the gold clasp and the authority of a doctorate before they have sweated at hard labor to the age of thirty or more, greatly reduced their patrimony, and ruined their health. To this, must we not add another ten years at least before they can establish the reputation and record of accomplishments necessary to make venal use of their scholarly learning? Not less than forty years have been lost before these covetous men can possibly earn money, at the last period of life, for how many men can you mention to me who even attain this age? How many out of a thousand men do you think, even without the anxiety of a scholar's life, even without the concerns that oppress his spirit, even leading a carefree and happy life, live beyond forty? If few among those who lead an easy life do so, surely you will find many fewer quattrogenerian scholars. For none of them is by nature so robust that the labors, long hours, and other harmful conditions in which they work do not nearly destroy them. The health of studious men is fragile, their life precarious, their lifespan necessarily short.

It will help to make the argument clearer if we reduce the issue to numbers. Men of mature judgment, whom I have asked from time to time how many men out of a thousand they think arrive at forty, usually, and in my opinion correctly, say that not more than three hundred out of a thousand men arrive at thirty, let alone at forty. They also say that it is rarely possible for a man under forty to provide properly for a family. Such was the answer they gave when I asked them. Hence, not to pass too lightly over this point, which is central to the subject of our discourse, let us go over our calculation of life-chances to select those men of letters who are able at a certain age to earn considerable wealth; then, if we find ourselves longing for lucre, let us realize how we must live, what proportion of learned men we must belong to, and what eminence we must first attain. Let us make the attempt.

Of the three hundred students of letters whose lives are prolonged to the age of thirty, I ask you how many are so free of misfortune during their whole lives, so spared from everyday evils and injuries, and so endowed with sufficiency, comfort and freedom, that they never have to break off their studies because of some cluster of disturbing events, but can in time reach the highest pinnacle of knowledge? Don't we know how full and ample are the ideas found in all the arts and how feeble is human intelligence to cultivate that vastness? Our reason and our mortal faculties may, in the course of events, become faltering and weak in the face of fortune's blows and the intrigues of men, which can make it difficult indeed to become outstandingly skillful in any art but surely most difficult, it seems to me, to take in the whole mass (so to speak) of learning. Let us then come to a consensus as to how many of our three hundred long-lived persons will not be driven by various misfortunes to end their studies and desert the field of letters or at least to interrupt their work. To decide correctly we should perhaps first consider how many cases of abandoned studies we know, a huge almost uncountable number, then remember how much easier it is for an event to put a stop to the student's persistence in his work than for him deliberately to take it up again later. If you reply that nothing ever makes you interrupt your literary work, surely you are either excessively fortunate or not much of a scholar; for in every sort of life we see every day that our studies, labors, and projects are interrupted by strokes of fortune and by various happenings. The impact of war, local outbreaks of disease and sometimes plague, the spinning of fortune's wheel, illnesses of mind or body, or such external pressures as poverty, attacks of enemies, animosities, and various other calamities can at times interrupt our career and so can injuries, losses, and problems (things life is full of) that demand our attention. For these reasons the wise men whom I queried on this subject gave the following answer: there are usually about a hundred out of three hundred whose studies survive these evils without detriment. We do not reject this number given by men of good judgment, though I myself would set my estimate lower. But let us be generous on this point. A hundred, then, out of a thousand students arrive, despite life's hazards and the influence of chance, at the point where they can make money from their learning.

We have already come down to a tenth of the whole group: I posited a thousand, we are left with a hundred. Again I ask: how many of this hundred do you think have the remarkable memory, intelligence, and talent required for the practice of higher learning? For not all who wish it, but only those to whom fate has given the ability as a special gift, are able to grasp the immense scope of learning. The memory and almost divine intelligence, which a certain special fate must lend to students of the highest arts, are granted by nature herself to very few. For if fate greatly endowed Hortensius with memory and Cicero with intelligence, it hardly granted any special glory of this kind to the many other rhetoricians of their time.

But we have strayed beyond the bounds of what we promised. We promised a bare discourse, honest and satisfied with truth alone, so let us avoid all amplification of our topic and get back to the point. Those who are not unsuited by their intelligence and powers of memory for the cultivation of learning are said by some to be many, by many to be rather few. We hold a position that takes something from both sides. I say that of one hundred who complete their studies unimpaired in thought, faculties, and functioning, ten may be gifted enough to attain praise for their scholarly work. But I don't know if even three of this number will be so attached to study, so in love with and eager for knowledge, so dedicated, so courageous and strong as to keep going despite all those troubles and anxieties which, as I have mentioned, go along with studies at every age. To the precariousness of man's fate, the uncertainty of fortune's gifts, and the frailty of human nature, if we add the extreme labors required by intellectual work, labors which, as I have been saying, are immense and cannot permit of interruption, who do you think is so bent on making money as not to put his very life first? This therefore will be our final computation, that out of a thousand men who turn naturally to study, three, by the time they reach forty, will still have enough capacity, spirit, intelligence, strength, and determination to earn riches by their intellectual work. And these, it is quite obvious, even if they perform remarkable intellectual work, will be old before they are able by their earnings to render their family glorious and wealthy. Of these perhaps we may say with Cato: they have worked hard to be wealthy among the shades. Thus, if there is a man of learning who is well-to-do during his lifetime, he should give the credit to fortune, not to virtue, and should know that his wealth is not the reward of his meritorious labors but of the largesse or rather the stupidity of fortune, for she, who in other matters usually scorns all the good, has been pleased, contrary to her custom, to be generous with him.

And how shall we rank this further hardship, possibly the worst, which befalls men of learning, that people never ask who among them has been most constant or most modest or has shown most integrity, but debate instead who is pushiest in public debates, most hardened in intrigue and in the concocting of legal frauds, sharpest, most audacious, most shameless? As if, indeed, it were known that the good are all ignorant when it comes to extorting money and inept when it comes to arguing a case. Yet if we judged correctly what is the expertise of highly educated men, perhaps flattery, sarcasm, and unscrupulous cunning would not outweigh the knowledge possessed by men of modesty and candor. Yet, at present the crowd is more pleased with malice than with righteousness, with deception, frivolity, and insolence than with humane and modest conduct, and it is the crowd without whose approval the man of learning can never escape poverty. The crowd, unable itself to beat the cunning bent on conquest and pillage with which their masters enter into lawsuits, when they see schemer colliding with schemer, glorify the one who wins by more successful scheming. Thus, if an unscrupulous learned legalist takes up an unjust case, they will call him a great master, the best of men, and a great friend. They have come to think deception a virtue, they admire the art of creating a mask and a false image as a remarkable mobilization of knowledge, and they believe that malice and wickedness and deliberate misinformation are derived from recondite knowledge. When a man is good and just and holy, when he argues cases for the merit they have in terms of justice and equity, when he stands for law and truth, not employing deceit and audacious lies, not shifting his allegiance at will, not hoping to win for the sake of money, but fighting for the sake of honor, they call him useless, ignorant, and a loser of cases. They never waver in their hatred of sincerity, never stop drawing people away from virtue, so that not only the venal, but even men who only want to earn their daily bread by their hard-won knowledge, are driven to the kind of betrayal of decency I have described. Men of learning who are greedy for wealth gain it (as we see with our own eyes) by avarice and crime when cunning and deceit are called for, while good and straight-forward men are left without clients. O cruel fate of studious men! What is their prime misfortune? The labors of a thousand men, their innumerable worries, their excessively long nights of work, the incredible labor that grows from day to day will bear some fruit for not more than three of them, and those fruits belong to the one who practices deceit, to the one who, to force fortune's favor, subordinates intelligence to cunning, intellect to mendacity, and his life to habitual vileness, the one who knows little but is called learned, whom the arrogant judgment of the ignorant crowd singles out for esteem. Thus a single opponent of all good learning, an enemy of good customs, one who condemns just causes and is prepared to commit any crime or outrage, seizes by his effrontery and presumption the wealth due to all the others, by his grasping overshadows the good name of all the rest, and by his ambition suppresses their name and fame. O hard reality that, of a thousand men who study, hardly one, and that one precisely the most iniquitous, attains to wealth! All you others, if you remain decent and honest, will be beggars, and even if dishonest, still may not be able to gain riches. For fortune, as is well known, does not smile consistently on all.

Because of these circumstances we must consider anyone who devotes himself to learning in the hope of wealth extremely foolish. For the services of learned men that lead to pay are either dishonest or servile. Further, as you have seen, the rewards, whatever they may be, trickle in meager and late, to only a few and not to the good, while even if they were large and honorable, they certainly would not be sufficient to cover previous expenditures.

What do shrewd observers say on this subject? Will they deny the truth of what I have said? I don't think they'll dare to contradict the true and well-known points of fact I have raised, but perhaps they will bring up a rich man who has some semblance of learning, and ask: "Why don't I think it would be possible for other scholars to become rich?" And if I chance to reply that the man they have mentioned gained his wealth by evil means, obviously I am hateful for having judged negatively of my colleague. If I say men like this are few and far between, perhaps they will say: "Given the minuscule number of the learned, even one is enough." They will mention all those who pursue learning for the sake of gain as evidence against me and as critics who do not agree with me.

Let me, therefore, restate my points most briefly here and again illuminate this issue of our wealth, for I think it will help to discourage the money-hungry students from an imprudent choice. I beg them to put aside their greed for money (if, by any chance, they have such feelings) and take a moment to read our arguments. If they do, they will never again approach books and knowledge without having made up their mind to scorn such acquisitiveness. So let us get to the point.

It is clear that for all the multitude of studious men who have distinguished themselves in the almost infinitely varied fields of knowledge, there are only three professions that will bring monetary reward. One is the profession of those who record cases and contracts, another, of those who are masters of jurisprudence, and the third, of those who treat the sick; all the rest it seems to me are not more known for their erudition than for their poverty. And that is not unfair, for only the arts that bring physical or material benefits are created and adapted to make money; while the arts that nourish spirit and mind lead to something else, something greater that is incorruptible and eternal. If you deny this, I ask you: have you found that grammarians, writers, and philosophers do not devote much effort to their work? Then let me ask: how many of these have you found who were rich? Haven't you noticed that almost all of these forms of learning go around begging for teaching positions in private households? I'll tell you what you might well answer: that philosophers despise wealth as an ultimate evil, so they deserve to be penniless and wretched. The three mentioned above, however, the scribe, the physician, and the lawyer, believe and teach that learning is superior and useful to the extent that it brings practical advantage. Other knowledge, of the mind, of the nature of things, of the ways of mankind, and of other important and beautiful matters, is despised and rejected in an ignorant and ugly way by the people of the city. Only venal learning is prized.

But I will never value wealth of these three kinds so highly that I do not find more worthy those who, for the sake of wisdom, bear poverty with fortitude. Even scribes, I have noticed, if they are really honest, are more commonly poor than the pettifoggers and informers among them; indeed I doubt whether there is any wealth in that profession not tainted by fraud and treachery. I dare say this with due respect to the good ones, for if one speaks up against the bad ones, one should be understood to favor the good. In the case of unscrupulous scribes, I think that we can believe their evil reputation and that they are even worse than people think. A sign of their utmost wickedness is the way they are always walking around without a pen behind the ear. They are not able to show their profession along with their wealth, for everyone knows how little gold flows from the scribal pen. So if a scribe does not wish to admit to theft and fraud, he must give the impression of poverty. Let others think what they like about scrupulous and unscrupulous notaries; to me it is implausible that any of them grows wealthy from the small fees he can charge for simply writing up documents.

Of medical men I would speak at more length; did I not see many good men and good doctors wrestling hard and bitterly with poverty, yet always ready to struggle on? The general public, however, takes the view that medical men, for the sake of money, wish for and follow precisely the things that other men consider sad and horrible, like wounds, disease, plague, and death. I leave it to the judgment of others whether, in making a fairly large income from these horrible things, they live avaricious, cruel, and desperate lives. I must touch lightly on this subject for the sake of brevity and also to avoid seeming to dwell too much on things that could bring disgrace on learning. So let me say nothing of fraud, betrayal of trust, false witness, corruption of contracts, and alteration of wills, and likewise omit discussion of the administration of poisons, augmentation of fevers, use of drugs and medications that make illnesses worse, and let me cover with silence all the other wicked and base things that are done by money-hungry scribes and doctors. Nor shall we discuss how the work of greedy scribes and doctors exposes them to bitter enmities and to infectious vapors. It would be offensive to linger over servile, obscene, and sordid work. A true intelligence and one raised by the teachings of the great writers to nobility of spirit surely could not and would not desire wealth obtained by vileness. Excellent minds prefer a moral life to riches. The truly learned despise crime and dishonor more than poverty. No one is so dense that he does not utterly despise the shameful, nefarious enslavement of greedy scribes and physicians.

Other men whom we consider slaves are taken prisoner in war or captured by pirates and go involuntarily into servitude, but physicians and scribes choose by an impulse of their own to become slaves. Slaves try to win the favor of their masters and thus attain liberty, working hard and loyally, as honorably as they can. But notaries and physicians in order to gain money do not refuse to carry out the vilest tasks. Slaves are willing to face danger and even death for the well-being of their masters, whether because they hope for freedom or because they appreciate the care and love they have received, but physicians and scribes willingly and greedily take on quarrels, diseases, contagion, and danger of death for a stranger, simply because they are attracted to the transaction by a little heap of coins.

What can I say of our lawyers that is truly good? What can I say in praise of canon law and civil law? For it is commonly said that these disciplines bring grain, while the other arts all gather only straw. Good gods! Big piles of documents, fat manuscripts, heavy portfolios (and how heavy, for god's sake!) become a complex apparatus that would bring anyone who took it to the tavern near the civic buildings a lot more money, if he charged the customers admission, than lawyers receive from their clients, for all their formal and organized pomp and for all the books and libraries of books on shelves in their houses. Just think: do you suppose anyone has the financial resources to purchase all those books without using up his whole fortune and more, and wouldn't it be the greatest folly to pursue wealth by spending so much? Aren't people who want to gain wealth by buying so many books with such an expenditure of money very much like the men Caesar described as fishing with hooks of gold? It is folly not only to want to pursue wealth by spending so much money but also to expend for that purpose such efforts and such enormous amounts of time.

"Tomorrow," says the client, "you must plead my case," and he gives you a modest sum, the rest being promised for later. Whatever is offered, you accept it and spend the whole night looking into books by the light of a lantern, with freezing feet and hands, looking for fantasms, thinking over stratagems and all that is in the books, bringing anxiety, weariness, hunger, and cold on yourself. The next day, you bring to the case a hoarse voice, a twisted neck, red and watery eyes, and a spirit not less thirsty and anxious for money than eager and willing to inflict harm. And you recite at the top of your lungs paragraphs and terms from the law woven into endless highly detailed arguments. You burst all the seams of your miserable heart; you are not afraid, for the sake of payment, to fight and quibble with the most powerful and eminent citizens. They threaten you, revile you, swear at you, cast blame on you. Unhappy man, you expose your reputation and your back to all this for the sake of money.

That's how it goes, doesn't it, when they labor for the money they want, when they proclaim and exclaim, when they suffer malice for a price, plead the cause of others, enter threateningly into their quarrels, and do all the things that this order of the educated known as lawyers consider appropriate, anything in fact that may bring monetary gain. Don't they even see how they are placed in public and horrible slavery? What a way to make money! These things not only fail to make them rich but actually ruin their families, even if their fathers were rich, make enemies, and, with the greatest expenditure of labor, involve them in servile bargains.

But perhaps someone will object as follows: Isn't it true that when men return home after years of study, they have enough authority to gain favor in society and to acquire wealthy wives? No one is so stupid that he doesn't want a connection to learned and famous men.

To this one might quite appropriately reply: How could a man of learning, unless he was crazy, choose to enslave himself just for the sake of money? A wise man desires freedom above all things, and more than anything, he avoids any kind of slavery, but especially slavery to a woman.[23] Any kind of servitude must be totally alien to one who cherishes wisdom; how wrong it is, then, for knowledge to give us authority so that we can enter something we consider honorable servitude. We should renounce the authority and reverence attached to learning rather than willingly appear to choose slavery for the sake of money. Anyone whose mind and inner counsels would rather take wealth with servitude than glory with liberty merits no authority at all. Yet what could be clearer than one's own servitude indeed, in serving another's purposes, pleading another's case, and making the quarrels of others one's own? What is clearer than that those who pursue big dowries willingly do just that? Don't we know how lawsuits unceasingly and steadily consume the energy of relatives, of relatives of relatives, and of their friends; don't we know that these people will ask for the unpaid labor and assistance of the learned one in their midst? Who would deny, moreover, that it is vilest servitude to submit to the assaults of a wife who is always talking about and insisting on her family's wealth and importance? That kind of thing always accompanies lavish dowries. Poor wretch! For the race of women is stupid, arrogant, quarrelsome, bold, insolent, and by nature aggressive.

In this sort of marriage what sort of wife do you think you will get? Spoiled by consciousness of her wealth, she will spend more than you, or rather she, can afford. Having been raised in luxury she will go wild with her abundance of ready money. Your wife will impose numerous rules on your conduct and frequently accuse you of being nothing, o sage, without her wealth. But it is more helpful not to speak of the nature and folly of women than once again to pour out, as it were, the endless and familiar litany. I only want to make sure it is accepted that, as they say, nothing is more unbearable than a wealthy woman.[24] Therefore, let us scholars not become so interested in gaining wealth through dowries that we do not despise servitude more than poverty!

Let us grant for a moment, however, that, as they claim, it would be suitable for men of learning to gain wealth by marriage. Who would dare most improperly to counsel a fortunate and wealthy mother to give a virgin daughter with a large dowry to a penniless scholar? Won't the mother say: "No indeed, I forbid our daughter's being given to this half-alive, rude, and gloomy man of letters?" Won't she also declare: "I want my daughter to be given a man, not a teacher?" And the girl herself, asked her opinion on her future, won't she say the same as her mother, her mind being inclined towards some other suitor and desiring for herself something other than an ample supply of philosophical sayings? And won't her brothers prefer a family connection with someone charming and urbane? So our scholar will be sent off, disgraced by the judgment and opinion of the mother, the brothers, and the girl herself.

Why am I lingering on this point, what if impoverished scholars do strive to gain rich dowries? I ask you, aren't there wealthy men who won't reject a wealthy bride? Certainly there are. But if they exist, my dear scholar, I urge you to get away from them, keep them out of your life, with all your Minerva and Pallas Athena despise acquaintance with such persons. Do not invite comparison of a poor fellow with a wealthy one, nor of your pale and gloomy countenance with that of other young men. Do not expect your authority to matter to a girl more than good looks. Go away, flee, hide yourself in your library. An athletic, handsome, attractive, and charming young man will make sure with all his skill and ingenuity that you do not take away his beloved. You'll be laughed at, graceless and poorly clad scholar, if you compete in matrimonial matters with a nicely groomed and polished lover. And if you show up pomaded and painted, you will lose all the authority and dignity of a man of learning.

You will say I am hard, not wanting scholarly men to marry. I want to be anything but cruel to scholars, yet not so merciful as to spare them the burden of marriage entirely. What sort of wife then, do I think a learned man should take? First, I advise any poor man to avoid marriage with a poor woman, for that is the ultimate evil. Second, I warn him not to desire a young female, for youth is an age unfavorable to scholars and offers them little security, I know what I am talking about. But let's not give examples. Let the scholar choose some little elderly widow, then, who is less likely to look down on him than other women, for this sort of elderly widow is driven by her children's defiance and her neighbors' insults to display herself in public, wanting to attract a man by her money, either so that he may provide protection from her persecutory in-laws who drag her daily into the courts, or so that she may be able to relax at home without anxiety and loneliness. And learned men consider they have done well for themselves in getting this kind of dowry, even if it involves lawsuits and terrific enmities. If I seem to be joking in this discourse about matrimonial matters, just call to mind the wives of learned men you know, consider their ages and dowries, to say nothing of their faithfulness.

It is important to remember how meager are the monetary rewards of scholarship, how slow, precarious, and paltry, and to keep firmly in mind what I have said about the enormous expenses involved, how heavy and constant these are, and how harmful to domestic arrangements. All these considerations will show, I think, that book learning is not of the slightest use for gaining wealth, but just the opposite, a great financial drain.

So now I think I have fulfilled the purpose of the first two parts of my argument. If I had any doubt that I have made my point, I would give another direction to this discourse and show the servile and cowardly spirit of the man who undertakes scholarly labors for the sake of monetary reward. Nor would I fail to point out that excellent and learned minds must value the height and splendor of their honor and intellect rather than covetousness and avarice. I could linger and luxuriate in this area, just to show my rhetorical powers or to gain glory by my eloquence, which is obviously very small, or to give more proof of my wide knowledge. For this is material that is easy, ample, and spacious, and anybody could expound it easily with much rhetorical embellishment. But it would be pointless and have no relevance to our purpose to wander on, polishing the presentation of well-known and much approved ideas.

For who is so ignorant that he would not describe this kind of thing as morally vile: to use the arts as compliant servants of avarice and greed, arts that are meant to cure and eliminate diseases of the spirit such as avarice, greed, and lust, and to develop and strengthen, in the soul which inclines toward evil, love of liberty, a sense of honor, nobility of spirit, and disdain for transitory things? To allow an intellect filled with the beauty of the disciplines to be crushed and ruined by the weight of shameful conduct? It is obviously contrary to our duty and disgraceful for anyone, including men of letters, not to lift up the soul as much as possible to what is honorable and good, worse to sink into avarice and disgrace, worst for a wise man to be guided by the attraction of transitory things. It is very bad to chase after wealth by usurpation of the authority of learning, worse not to use one's strengths in defense of one's honor and liberty, worst to participate in unscrupulous monetary transactions. But let us not talk about all this, since I gave myself the task of going into nothing unnecessary to my argument and promised to be concise, as so far I have been—as concise as I could be. For this, as you have seen, has been a succinct and closely articulated presentation. So it will continue to be, also, insofar as the magnitude of the subject permits: very easy to follow and short.

v.

I have said that from the study of letters one does not garner pleasures or attain wealth; now it seems I should address myself to the prestige and honors given to men of learning. It is perfectly obvious that honors in full measure are their due. For if honor is properly given as a prize for merit, who deserves it more? Could anyone deny, could anyone be so monstrous as to reject this truth: that bringing progress to the arts through arduous and continuous labor, augmenting one's goodness and wisdom by devoting every age to study, spurning all pleasant distractions, rejecting all one's appetites, pouring out energy and money, thus giving up one's time and fortune to help and benefit the human race, deserves universal gratitude? Could anyone be so monstrous as to deny that these are precious gifts, that we learn from books to understand the noble arts, to strengthen good institutions, to appreciate excellent morals, and to cherish wisdom, and that therefore men of learning should rank above all other men and all kinds of men? The universal understanding is that men of learning should not be slighted.

We recognize that man surpasses all other living things in many ways, but most of all in that special gift which is knowledge and reason, that ability which can convince us that the minds of men are not in essence different from the minds of heavenly beings. Indeed, we see that all the things that move on earth and in the sea are cultivated and made useful in their abundance by the natural intelligence of men. Everyone admits that man is by nature the most honored of all living beings and their king. In view of which, if a man possesses reason or mind, which nature has set up as the lord of all things, in its most complete form, perfected by education, cultivated and polished by study and application, and is therefore much superior to others in reason and intelligence, doesn't this most excellent of mortals deserve the greatest honors and the reverence of all? God himself, who is highest in an infinity of other ways, is divine in part, and perhaps especially, because of his perfect discernment of good and evil, his perfect ability to choose the best and to rule the world according to reason and providence; if a man, then, manifests his knowledge and wide reading in this divine way, shouldn't he of all men receive almost divine honors, shouldn't he rank highest?

Why then should the knightly order take precedence over learned men in public processions? What knight is comparable to a sage? What an act of impudence to put a rude, ignorant, and usually licentious soldier ahead of all learned men! This custom began, I think, not by our ancestors instituting it deliberately, but by those very warriors putting themselves boldly and insolently in front. Unless indeed our ancestors considered knowledge less worthy of honor than gold! By some perverse reasoning, some evil custom, some unjust privilege, a soldier devoid of virtue, morality, and the splendor of wisdom, who wishes only to be noted for his accumulation of jewels and gold, takes precedence over a learned man who, through virtue, intelligence, knowledge, and understanding of books and of the highest things, has attained a character that is moderate and pure. Let us leave this point regarding the wrongful elevation of soldiers, however, though indeed it is not irrelevant to our subject. Let us admit, moreover, that the military function is something of public value, that the soldier's own task and office are not a trivial business: his job is, with his own wealth, resources, and weapons, to protect, shield, and defend virgins, widows, the poor and defenseless, orphans and all poor people, all the afflicted of any kind, as well as the whole republic. That is how I see the duty of the military, and others may judge how conscientiously knights perform it and to what extent, therefore, they ought to be honored. No one can deny, however, that learned men by their studies are very useful to the republic, to the poor, and even to the wealthiest citizens, so who could give any reason for somehow putting the stupid ahead of the wise, the ignorant ahead of the knowledgeable, the useless ahead of the helpful, the lazy ahead of the active and long-deserving?

Nor is it only the military who defraud men of learning of status, for the learned are in fact widely despised. Can you show me any citizen somewhat notable for wealth and status who does not wish to be thought the best in every way? Can you show me one wealthy man who does not scorn poverty and, therefore, inwardly despises the studies and arts and knowledge of poor men? Where would you find a wealthy man so scrupulous that he does not consider it his right to be more regarded for his fortune than others for their virtue?

"Why on earth," the wealthy ask, "should you prefer that learned man to me? Is not our country one and the same? Do you suppose my relatives, family, and clan are inferior to his? Does my perhaps not knowing as much grammar make my opinion and my vote in the senate count for less? To us the city is free, and so is our mind. We are free to speak in our mother tongue among ourselves, and we speak it well enough not to be reduced to helpless silence. Let the rhetorician delight in the words of his precious authors. We tend to matters of business and acquire wealth, so our opinion in the senate counts more. I know we succeed better than any literary scholar with his heavy rhetorical phrasing in establishing the authority of our wealth. We offer golden opinions, he offers opinions with laurels, and the laurel surrenders to the gold.

"You who take up the cause of study, now stop glorifying the man of learning so much," they say. "Why should I stand up in his presence? Why should I step aside for him on the street? Why take off my hat? What is my business with him? So he knows books, what's that to me? Let him direct the games and instruct the children. So he is able to cite the law, what's that to me? Let him shout and proclaim, write down things that are said, cheat widows, prey on those who have lawsuits, let him confuse his little clients, let him advertise his ability to counsel citizens. The town that's bereft of these advisers is better off than the one that's full of them. If he professes medicine, what's that to me? Let him cure the drunken, the gluttons, the big consumers, let him sell as many drugs and perform as many filthy services as he can, what do I care? If he is learned in theology, what do I care? Let him please old widows with his long sermons, let him rave in the pulpits if he wants to, what do I care? What harm can come to that man of learning: he knows it all, has learned everything, exhibits universal understanding, so what? If I ever need one of them, for a single coin I can make him work three days and nights without stopping.

"Let them be happy with their empty discussions, but not bring their petty squabbles before the public. Better than that, let them return to the lanterns they stink of. And after that, dear gods, with this plague of men out of sight, there will not be the strife of litigants, the calumnies uttered in court. Quarrels and lawsuits will cease and in the cities highest harmony will rule. Peace established among citizens will be unbroken. Not by eternal lawsuits, not by endless legal bickering, but under the guidance of fair and good nature, a certain simple equity will be discovered in every case."

These words, I call the gods to witness, I have heard too often from my fellow citizens, men who were neither obscure nor without distinction. And I have given them no response commensurate with my annoyance, lest they think me arrogant. For they were judging the question on the basis of ignorance, not guided by experience, nature, and a sense of justice, but by hatred and envy. It seemed better to be in a certain sense indulgent with them, who were refusing to acknowledge what they did not understand and vituperating against what they were unable to comprehend. All I would ask was, for my sake, to speak more moderately and gently of good men. But they would go on with their raving.

O mild-tempered self-restrained city! Who has not heard the same stuff again and again in every public place? Who, if he's not altogether crude and vile, can bear to listen to such men? Who that wants a bit of recognition, when he sees the utter indifference of wealthy men, will not begin to wish for money rather than wealth of knowledge? What will he feel when he hears a scholar called a servant or a cook, if by chance, as sometimes happens, he leaves his books to approach a group of citizens without having dressed up? If he mentions with some passion the thoughts that he has developed in reading, he may be called a marble bull or a ranter. An ambitious yapper, they will call him, if he shows some delight in a public display of eloquence and learned language. Indeed, to ask for any public honors and authority in this situation is to bring down the authority and dignity of learning still more.

As far as honors go, we scholarly men are better off if we are dull rather than intelligent. For the custom of our fellow citizens is to laugh at the dull and make fun of them, but the fiery and active minds they describe as wicked and greedy, as a kind of men whom one should avoid, because with both natural intelligence and trained cunning they will do harm and hatch evil plots. So how will you, a learned man, present yourself? If you show simplicity, they say you are good but unsophisticated and useless. If you show that you are polished and discriminating, they will brand you malicious.

What else shall I say of the way our people behave towards men of learning? It seems to be the nature of men in cities to be big talkers and nasty gossips, but they are most brazen and evil-minded in our Tuscan towns. There they mock everyone, defer to no one, speak wildly, and behave with insolence. I think I should actually give some credit for this to our people and to Tuscany. In the Tuscan cities, because of their ancient liberty, it is permitted to say and do things which, to those raised under tyrants, would seem carelessly spoken or intemperately done. It is the glory of liberty, and its consequence, that, as long as you obey the laws, you can choose your own pleasures and your own course.

But let us return to our populace, who have always given the highest honors to gold and wealth. Indeed, it is no mystery why the crowd is moved, not so much by virtue as by outward splendor. For the ignorant are attracted by the things they can see with their eyes while those things that can and ought to enlighten them do not move them. So the ignorant desire the riches they can see and disregard the wisdom they do not have, follow after property and despise virtue. The wealthy man appears in public with a long train of friends and servants, expressing unmistakably by face and gestures that he has what it takes to help or harm other people. To the one whose wealth engages their greed, the crowd offers applause as soon as they see his face and figure. As he comes nearer, they rise up instantly, for they suppose and expect that a man of such outstanding fortune should be made much of. Understandably enough, they put a man from whom they hope to get favors and money before any and all men of learning. Fueled by greed, then, especially in our city, the idea has flourished that highest honors should go only to the wealthy and fortunate, while accomplished scholars are considered objects of little future utility. Why not despise them indeed? I shall omit all sorts of further shameful insults the populace hurls at scholarly men.

But let's not omit this one: they don't see why they should glorify our studious men who obviously omit in their way of life everything that is necessary for a good and happy life. "You don't practice what you preach," they say. "Thanks to books you know everything, thanks to the great and divine knowledge you gain by your intellectual labors there's nothing you don't know. Why then, are you learned fellows such stupid people? How crazy do you have to be not to learn, first of all, how to be comfortable? Aren't you ashamed of your wretched poverty? Why should we, for our part, make much of the knowledge you offer, when more of you seem hungry and thirsty than wise? Learn first to free yourselves from poverty, you men of learning (if you really want to seem wise) and then you'll earn praise for your lives."

For the most part, as you see, learned men are held up to ridicule by every order of society, mocked by the crowd, laughed at by everybody, despised by many, and most despised when they have too little cash. If they happen to be well off (which is most rare) they know quite well that people honor them, not for their knowledge of books, but for their money, not for their virtue, but for their good luck. One observes how people get up, how they make way or show courtesy only when their eyes have first raked over the splendor of a scholar's golden toga; if the gold isn't there, if you take off the robe, they disregard you. This is the way men of learning discover how the world works: if your clothes are fancy, you are highly honored; riches, to most people, merit respect and attention, and no one, however prudent, experienced, and outstanding for his knowledge and understanding of the highest things, will be able to give the crowd anything it admires and rewards with praise unless he enjoys popularity for his money and possessions.

Perhaps we should consider such things as public office, positions in legations and in the government to be greater honors than foremost rank in a procession or signs of deference in the street, but precisely these things, as we know too well, have long been claimed for the most part by gold.

Perhaps the rulers of the republic seem perfectly and rightfully placed in a position of high honor, being morally and practically of tested worth, men whom the republic has trusted with its own great weight because of their faith and diligence. I cannot persuade myself that the republic needs book learning in its magistrates more than the practical knowledge gained by long experience and practice. I think I should clarify this point briefly here. I have noticed that, in fact, the government rarely holds meetings to discuss the heavens and the planets, and never to discuss the nature of the gods, procreation, and the soul. Discussions in the senate are sure to deal with war and peace, revenues and costs, the regulation and defense of all aspects of civic life, and so they rely, not on philosophical reading, but on custom and experience. I don't hear them debate about the seven planets, or about the wandering stars, or what can be known of the sun and moon, so really, the study of the liberal arts ought to be segregated and kept out of the courts and government offices. Further, those who consider themselves scholars would be better off if they fled such places entirely and remained content with their books, for they earn no public respect there. If, however, they really desire participation in public life, let them take as much of a role as is proper to one neither called to it nor, on the other hand, excluded. Let them work on writing up and witnessing terms of peace and alliance. Let them leave the rest of public affairs to the very knowledgeable and very virtuous men who have by their oath, at the will and command of the people, taken on the responsibility.

Men of learning, indeed, who do not want to appear to have more knowledge and experience in negotiation than in scholarship, will make themselves useful in their own tasks, editing the public records according to what they saw themselves or heard from competent witnesses. Anyone who really wants to do the wise thing, in short, should flee all administrative work. It is not easy to describe how damaging all public responsibilities generally are, first of all to any citizen who would rather be disentangled from business concerns and free, and second, in particular, to minds fully occupied with study of the arts and intellectual disciplines. Here are the disadvantages of government work: it distracts one's mind from one's private concerns, drags one into worry and envy, confronts one with enmities and dangers, loads one with cares, labors, and embittering difficulties. All these things obviously are harmful to anybody, including men of scholarly inclination, and are therefore prohibited terrain for minds that have attained tranquillity.

What is more, even if you have heard that once men of learning were held in high honor, esteem, and admiration, these days a different spirit rules, too many take up the study of books, and some are insolent, vile, and shameful. Today, while we see the most sacred scholarly studies infiltrated and disgraced by such dregs, the best and finest men, who at one time preserved the purity of the liberal arts, are driven to despise them. So they neglect these studies from which neither honor nor power can be obtained, and we have degenerated to the point where, not only men of outstanding nobility and authority neglect the study of books, but really no one takes them up except the most miserable and lazy people. Hunchbacks, people with running sores, twisted dwarfs, dolts, stutterers, men without spirit, and all the generally incompetent and noncompetitive are supposed scholars. Those whom other civic activities reject think they are suited to make use of a literary leisure: men whom insignificant little women turn down as husbands bind themselves to study. Those who are notable for intelligence, therefore, clearly see that they should put their energy into something more attractive and more advantageous, anything rather than scholarship.

Who can fail to see in all this that our citizens do not value education? Who can deny that the dignity and honor of learning has been ruined? Who cannot observe, as if painted before his eyes, the downfall and destruction of the noble disciplines and liberal arts? Who would not mourn for such a disaster, such a shipwreck of the literary arts? For storms and disasters have afflicted our way of life: almost no one pursues the noble disciplines for the sake of his own mind, a few do so for the sake of honor, and an infinite number out of greed and the hope of wealth.

Now all the liberal arts and sciences, established as sacred possessions of the mind, lie in a state of servitude. Law, theology, knowledge of nature, and knowledge of human conduct, as well as all other marvelous fields of study meant only for free men have been (oh hideous crime!) put up for sale as if on the auction block. Innumerable slave traders in the noble arts buzz around bidding for merchandise. From field and forest and from the very clods of earth and mud, there swarm a vast number of creatures, not men but beasts born to perform servile labors, who, abandoning their native countryside as unworthy, rush to sell and profane the disciplines. Oh plague of literacy! What is going on, that men who should be wielding a pickaxe or a pitchfork are disrespectfully handling books and words? Men meant to herd sheep and inhabit stables are discussing and judging the fortunes of humanity. Those who should be governing sheep with their staffs now hold the scepter as they sit among the magistrates. They have left their sheep not for the sake of a higher vocation but for a different image and place in society. Untouched by education, this bold and, as the poet says, gaping crowd has moved in; they aren't held back by any fear of disrepute, of dishonor, of moral filth, they are perfectly ready to perform any cruelty; tainted with every sort of crime and evil, undeterred by shame, by decency, by good education or the noble arts, they are guided in judging what is good and evil not by virtue and wisdom but by greed and avarice, equating poverty with misery and seeing wealth alone as the highest good, and these men write up contracts deciding the fortune, fame and the very life of innocent people. They don't hesitate, for the sake of profit, to bring plague and ruin on anyone at all. Bold and unscrupulous criminals, driven by greed for gold, they are afraid of nothing. The word, the noble arts, and sacred studies, are theirs to sell, theirs to turn into pelf. Knowledge of divine and human matters, guide to good conduct and true glory, discoverer and parent of the best things in life, once you ornamented the souls of men, cultivated intelligence, conferred glory, grace, and dignity; once you offered your wisdom to the republic and accustomed the whole world to act according to the highest forms of law and order. You, philosophy, mother of learning, I ask you, are you now supporting and serving the greed of the vilest and most degraded men?

But let us stop our lamentation about the calamity and destruction that have fallen on education, let us stop inquiring as to the cause of this degradation and downfall of study, for it is a vast subject and outside the scope of our undertaking. Let stand only what we have tried, briefly but truthfully, to demonstrate: that in devotion to books you will find much work, no pleasures, great expense, little profit, many difficulties, many dangers, and very little authority. In the exposition of these matters I have tried to be brief and have deliberately stated many points without fully discussing them, outlined many propositions without illustrating them, have presented many ideas without amplifying them. This I have done lest I appear to condemn in excessive detail that to which I have been more than a little devoted myself. I do not doubt that our discourse, which, though sparse, meager, and humble, has been consistently on the side of virtue, will go safely before the critical judgment of scholars. A discourse is sufficiently refined and ample, I think, that cannot be found to contain any lies or misrepresentations, sufficiently honorable if it lets no wickedness in. Let no one blame me, therefore, if I have chosen to appear not very eloquent rather than too sharp. Indeed, it is the furthest thing from my mind to disrespect the study of books. For love of these I have suffered great anxiety, labor, and discomfort. I have encountered injuries, losses, wounds, and calamities while I devoted myself completely to learning, to the point where even some who supported my life both financially and by their confidence in me were unhappy about it. And indeed I endured poverty, hostility, and violence that, as many know, was not minor or trivial, done to me just as my studies were about to bear fruit, and I was able to bear all this with a strong, upright and undivided spirit only because of my appreciation and love for study. And of course I chose to continue in this way of life not for pleasure and not for money, which I could have gained if I had transferred my activity from books to business. Indeed, as I lived on the resources of others, I might have put their considerable funds to whatever use I chose. Asking much from others, I could have been more generous in listening to their pleas. But knowledge, noble disciplines, and most abstruse arts were always worth more to me than all the gifts of fortune and all the advantages. Let no one think, therefore, that the things I have said here express toward study resentment or finicky disdain. These things are so obvious and clear that I need not belabor them with eloquence.

I hope, however, that our discourse may be of use to students in that they will hold on with all their sense and reason to what I have explained, and thus, with my help, if I have some effect, will study more diligently than ever, fully understanding that study does not offer pleasurable license nor meaningless transitory rewards. The noble arts, moreover, bring not any or at most a very meager harvest to men of evil disposition. Only utter fools, we think, opt for scholarship hoping for anything other than knowledge of the highest things. It is proper for those wise persons who rightly wish both to be and to seem learned, to burn with zeal for study, to read a great deal, and to consider it their primary mission to perfect not only their erudition but also their character. Let the spirit of the learned be aflame with desire of a certain kind, not for gold and goods, but for the right way to live and for wisdom. Let them seek in books, not so much the essential nature and causes of things as the nature and even the love of virtue and glory. Let them assiduously avoid idle pleasures, despise wealth, scorn ceremonies, try not to fear fortune, and focus only on achieving peace of mind, good conduct, virtue and wisdom, for here is almost all that the noble arts strive for. What we have found in the writings of our ancestors all tends in the same direction, toward freedom from errors, toward love of truth and simplicity. These two things are the foundation and the pillars of a good and happy life, and if these are well set and well built, we go on to build well both a virtuous character and reason, the companion of virtue. The mind then enjoys the gift of intelligence and wisdom, and the intellect unperturbed by changes of fortune stands victorious. In your practice of learning, therefore, seek after glorious wisdom, defend and preserve goodness with all your might. That is what the books themselves (if they could speak) would demand of you.

"Having squandered your health in long vigils, where are you going, young man? How will such labors be useful to you? What are you asking of us by all this diligence and zeal? What is the point of these wakeful hours, anxious strivings, and all this thinking? Do you seek some gratification from tormenting yourself with cares? Do you ever give yourself a rest? Do you hope for wealth, while you learn from us not to fear poverty? Or have you somehow overlooked the fact that nothing belonging to us is for sale? Let it be no secret to you, young man, that we are more inclined to have our lovers poor than rich. For we know by experience that no scholar has become wealthy but, immersed in the delights and luxuries that riches bring, he began to hate our presence and everything associated with us. So? Do you want power, honors, glory, and status? You are mistaken, young man, you are mistaken if you put public flattery and popularity above goodness, if you do not consider the game of fortune, the tumult of public life, the winds of popular favor far less important than knowledge and wisdom. Those things, which are transitory, unstable, fragile, full of pointless effort, rife with fears and suspicions, fraught with mishaps and downfalls, who would compare them to peace of mind and stability of character, as well as to the beauty of the noble disciplines? Can you have missed, young man, the fact that virtue is all around you when you are with us, that we love no greed, no arrogance, no passion, no spiritual flightiness, that we demand a spirit perfectly clear of any malice, of any shadow of evil? Don't you see, young man, what light and splendor the wisdom we are talking about bestows on those who are dedicated to us, how it tends to make them luminous and glorious? Consider the full remembrance of forgotten antiquity and its wisdom that you find in us, which can help you rise above and endure any attack or accident of fortune. Therefore let go of that greedy kind of mind, let go of this desire of your spirit for exalted status, flee from those false values of money, vain fame, and corrupt popularity that you introduce into your scholarly work. It is folly deliberately to pursue ends you cannot attain, but even more foolish to expend your energy for a kind of success which, if you are unable to attain it, will make you regret your wasted efforts, and if you do attain it, will make you ashamed of your corruption.

With us, you will expend more moderate labor and show a more exacting kind of virtue. From us, you will obtain not only knowledge of the teachings, which is rightly thought of as the companion of virtue, but with hope, reason, and thought you will become from day to day more imbued with perfect character. Learning and the arts give you this glorious thing: that you are free to aspire to wisdom. Virtue will bestow on you this divine gift: that you may reach peace of mind, praise, dignity, and happiness. For if, as you should, you put everything else second and strive for virtue, release from all vices will naturally occur and reputation and glory will follow. For virtue is pre-eminent and outstanding, being linked and integrated with a certain divine power by which we are released from all vices and errors. This brings us praise and honor and maintains our whole and permanent spiritual happiness and peace of mind. He who embraces this kind of virtue in his soul, his will, and his conduct, who remembers that solid and real goodness is not found in the judgment of the multitude but in elegance and splendor of mind, does not want to compromise with fortune. For him all the goods he possesses are found in himself, thanks to which he leads a life that is outstanding and blessed and similar to that of the gods. Since these things are so, young man, surrender to virtue. Judge fortune's gifts as none of them worthy of intense longing, none of them preferable to the goods of the spirit. For men who have proved their character nothing is worth pursuing except wisdom and virtue, nothing worth fearing and fleeing except ignorance and vice. If a man wishes to cultivate his mind, therefore, he will inevitably come to despise, hate, and abhor those filthy things called pleasures and those enemies of virtue known as luxury and riches, as well as all the other plagues that infest our life and our spirit, such as honors, elevated status, and grandeur. If you focus your energies consistently, young man, in the direction of the goals we have described, you will find that study is full of pleasure, a good way to attain praise, suited to win you glory and to bear the fruit of posterity and immortality."

Thus it is, Carlo, my brother, that we, like our forefathers, are aroused and uplifted by the exhortation and admonishment of the written word to pursue our studies in such a way as to prove our virtue to all and allow no one to doubt that our striving is for wisdom alone.

Notes

[1] The critical edition is by Laura Goggi Carotti, *De Commodis litterarum atque incommodis*, Leon Battista Alberti (Firenze: L. S. Olschki, 1976) and was preceded by a helpful bilingual edition by Giovanni Farris, *De Commodis litterarum atque incommodis, defunctus*, testo latino, traduzione italiana, introduzione e note a cura di Giovanni Farris (Milano: Marzorati, 1971). Series title: Pubblicazioni dell'Istituto di Lingua e Letteratura Italiana I.

[2] Friedrich Nietzsche, "Vom Nutzen und Nachtheil der Historie," Part Two of *Unzeitgemaessigen Betrachtungen* is known in English as "The Use and Abuse of History." *Nutzen und Nachtheil* is very close indeed to *De Commodis atque incommodis*.

[3] "The Life of Leon Battista Alberti," by himself, trans. by Renee Neu Watkins, *Italian Quarterly* XXX 17 (Summer 1989): 7.

[4] Ibid., p. 8.

[5] Girolamo Mancini, *Vita di Leon Battista Alberti*, (reprint of edition of 1911) (Rome: Bardi, 1967), p. 45.

[6] Ibid., p. 67 but see also note 3.

[7] "The Life of Leon Battista Albert," p. 8.

[8] Ibid., p. 8.

[9] Mancini, p. 70.

[10] "The Life Leon Battista Alberti," p. 8.

[11] Ibid., p. 8.

[12] The date of the treatise is now in dispute, but the arguments either way are necessarily speculative. Cf. Luca Boschetto, "Nuovi documenti su Carlo di Lorenzo degli Alberti e una proposta per la datazione del *De Commodis litterarum atque incommodis*," *Albertiana* I (1998): 43–60. Though we have no evidence that Alberti was there before 1432, he may have travelled to Florence in 1428–1430. If Alberti's direct observation of Florentine behavior in *De Com.* dates from 1432 or later, however, his very different treatment of the conflict between practicality and book-learning in *Della Famiglia* must show a different side of him, rather than a development. As to the evidence for the later date, Carlo's *Ephebie* is referred to in the dedication of the treatise, and a manuscript in Venice of that work is clearly from 1431–1432, but is it the original manuscript? If so, the dedicatory introduction would have to be of a later date, since it quotes from *Ephebie*, but is the rest of the work later as well? Was it really his cousin's son, Ricciardo, rather than his brother's possible son by the same name, that Alberti commemorated in a Latin note, referring to the birth of a "nepos"? The question arises because earlier scholars accepted the speculation that Battista rushed to Florence in 1429 (actually it

should be early 1430 by our system of dating) to see his newborn nephew. If we disregard both Carlo's son and 1428 as too early a date for the treatise, the contrast remains between Carlo's secular Florentine life employed in the Alberti business and Battista's choice of a life at the Curia which would allow him to follow his literary and artistic pursuits. The fact remains also that Alberti in the *Vita* assigned the treatise to his twenty-fourth year and, whether the date is precisely accurate or not, clearly relates it to his situation at the time he broke off his studies at the University of Bologna.

[13] Published by Richard Scholz, "Eine Humanistische Schilderung der Kurie 1438," *Quellenforschungen aus italienischen Archiven* 16 (1914): 116–53.

[14] Franco Borsi, *Leon Battista Alberti*, trans. Rudolf G. Carpanini (New York: Harper and Row), 1977, p. 10.

[15] Cf. Cecil Grayson, "Alberti e l'Antichita," *Albertiana* I (1998): 31–41.

[16] Dante, *Paradiso* XVI, pp. 49–72.

[17] "*Prestat enim et excellit virtus, nam ei coniuncta et complexa est divina quedam vis qua levamur a vitiis atque erroribus omnibus, quam laus, honor, integraque et permanens animi voluptas et quies subsequitur et persistit.*" Carotti, p. 115.

[18] The use of "parens" rather than "father" may refer to the fact that Lorenzo was both father and mother to his children after their mother died in 1406, when Battista was two and Carlo probably a little older. Lorenzo himself died in 1421, when Battista was seventeen. The exile of the Alberti family was rescinded in 1428, probably the year the present treatise was presented to Carlo.

[19] Occasionally Alberti slips from "I" to "we" (the singular to the plural or vice versa) for no apparent reason.

[20] These misfortunes are alluded to metaphorically in the *Intercoenales* and literally described, under the veil of anonymity, in the *Vita*.

[21] The definition is from Cicero, *Fin.* I.56, as cited by Carotti, p. 48.

[22] Dead sheep refers to parchment made of sheepskin.

[23] Giovanni Farris notes a possible source of this sentiment in Propertius *Eleg.* II.23–4.

[24] Farris identifies the remark as an echo of Juvenal *Sat.* II.6, 458.